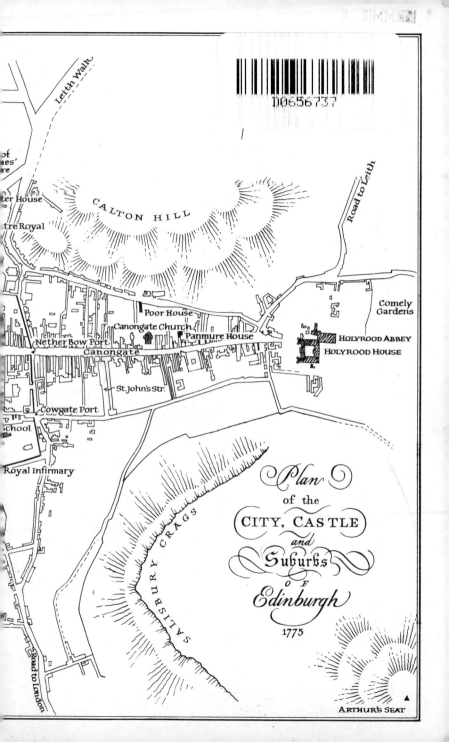

Letth Walk.

D0656737

CALTON HILL

Road to Leith

ter House

tre Royal

of
es'
re

Poor House

Canongate Church

Nether Bow Port

Panmure House

Canongate

Comely
Gardens

HOLYROOD ABBEY

HOLYROOD HOUSE

St. John's Str.

Cowgate Port

chool

Royal Infirmary

SALISBURY CRAGS

Plan
of the
CITY, CASTLE
and
Suburbs
OF
Edinburgh
1775

Road to London

ARTHUR'S SEAT

THEN AND THERE SERIES

GENERAL EDITOR

MARJORIE REEVES, M.A., PH.D.

Edinburgh in its Golden Age

WILLIAM K. RITCHIE, M.A.

Illustrated from contemporary sources

1724

LONGMANS

LONGMANS, GREEN AND CO LTD
48 Grosvenor Street, London W.1

*Associated companies, branches and representatives
throughout the world*

TO ISHBEL

ACKNOWLEDGEMENTS

The author would like to thank the staffs of Huntly House Museum, the Museum of Antiquities, the Scottish National Portrait Gallery and especially Mrs. Armstrong and staff of the Edinburgh Room, Edinburgh Public Library, for their help in preparing this book.

We are also grateful to the following for their permission to reproduce these illustrations: Country Life—page 65; Edinburgh Public Library—pages iv, 2, 4, 7, 8, 9, 10, 11, 12, 13, 28, 48, 51, 85, 87 and 92; M. Harris & Sons—page 25 top (L/H Chair); Francis C. Inglis & Son Ltd.—page 72; Mallett & Son (Antiques) Ltd.—page 25 top (except L/H Chair); Mansell Collection—pages 45 lower right, 83 and 101; Museum of Fine Arts, Boston—page 77; National Galleries of Scotland—pages 20, 35, 42, 46, 59, 61, 64, 67, 71 and 81; National Monuments Record of Scotland—pages 29, 30 and 99; National Museum of Antiquities, Scotland—pages 19, 23 lower, 25 lower, 37, 38 and 43; Radio Times Hulton Picture Library—page 79; Scottish National Portrait Gallery—pages 44 right and 96.

The 'Gentleman of the 1770s' on page 45 is by permission of the Duke of Argyle, from his collection in the Scottish National Portrait Gallery; and the photograph on page 94 is Crown Copyright Reserved. The illustration on page 36 is reproduced from Colston: 'Edinburgh & District Water Supply;' that on page 44 left from Kay's 'Edinburgh Portraits', and those on pages 5, 6, 22, 23 top, 27 and 53 are all from Grant: 'Old and New Edinburgh'. The plan on pages 14-15 has been redrawn from the original in Huntly House, and the map on the front endpaper is from the original in Edinburgh Public Library.

PRINTED IN GREAT BRITAIN BY
E. J. ARNOLD AND SON LIMITED
LEEDS

CONTENTS

TO THE READER

Look carefully at these two maps. Notice the difference between them. They show two parts of the same city. In the one

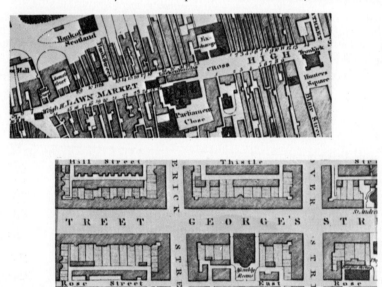

the houses are crowded together in narrow streets. In the other the houses are neatly spaced out and the streets are regular. The first is a map of the old part of the town. The houses here were put up when they were needed and the people lived very close together. In the second map we see a more recent part, with houses and streets that were all carefully worked out according to a plan and then built. We call this Town-planning. All houses and streets are built like this now. Sometimes whole towns—houses, streets, schools, shops and factories—are planned first and then put up. They are called New Towns. Crawley, East Kilbride, Glenrothes and Harlow are all examples.

Two hundred years ago town-planning was new. In Edinburgh a New Town grew up beside the old one. You have been looking at maps of the city. The first house was started in 1767 and building the rest went on for about sixty years. This was a time when many poets, artists and writers lived in Edinburgh. There were so many that some people said that the city was like ancient Athens in its Golden Age. They called it the Athens of the North and spoke of the Athenian Age because of Edinburgh's fine buildings and famous men.

This book describes what it was like to live in Edinburgh then. It tells about some of the men who made the city famous and also about the great events of the time—revolutions and wars—and how they affected the people of Edinburgh in its Golden Age.

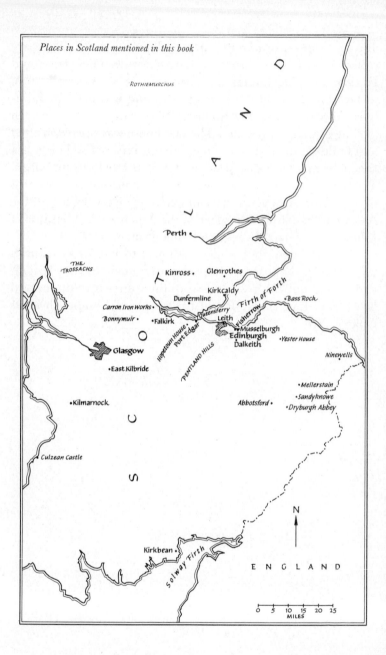

Places in Scotland mentioned in this book

ROTHIEMURCHUS

L A N D

Perth

THE TROSSACHS

Kinross • Glenrothes

Kirkcaldy

Carron Iron Works • Dunfermline

Bonnymuir • Falkirk

Firth of Forth Bass Rock

Queensferry Leith Fisherrow

Hopetoun House Musselburgh

Port Edgar Edinburgh

Glasgow Dalkeith

O Yester House

East Kilbride PENTLAND HILLS

Ninewells

Mellerstain

Kilmarnock Abbotsford • Sandyknowe

Dryburgh Abbey

S C

Culzean Castle

N

Kirkbean

Solway Firth

E N G L A N D

0 5 10 15 20 25
MILES

1 Stranger in Town

It was already dark one November evening when two horse-men were reaching their destination, tired and hungry. As their horses picked their way along the rutted tracks of the main road into town, the two companions looked forward to a warm meal and a comfortable night's rest at an inn. They found one, but to their disgust, what was called an inn in those parts was fit only for stabling horses. A disappointing start to a holiday in Edinburgh!

Edward Topham was one of these travellers. In the winter of 1774 this young Englishman, aged twenty-four, spent about six months in the Scottish capital with his friend Paul Jodrell. He wrote many letters to his friends in London and Paris, telling them about his experiences. These letters give us an idea of what life in Edinburgh was like at the time. He had just returned from his Grand Tour, which means he had been spending a few years on the Continent, visiting places of interest in cities like Paris, Geneva and Rome. It was quite common for well-to-do parents to send their sons on such a journey to finish off their education before they settled down in some profession. A tutor usually went as well, to see that the young man did some reading; but it was not all hard study; there was a great deal of fun on the way.

Edward Topham had now chosen to come to Scotland to see what the country was like. This must have been an unusual thing for Englishmen to do, for he found many people in Edinburgh asking why he had come. He and his friend were taken at first for actors or dancing-masters. Yet perhaps the fashion of English travellers visiting Scotland was growing, for in the 'Scots Magazine' of 1772 we can read an article beginning in this way:

'It is now become fashionable among the English to make

Edinburgh from the South

a tour into Scotland for some weeks and months; and there is a moral certainty of this fashion increasing, as the foolish prejudices against the country and its inhabitants daily decrease. But it is to be regretted that an intelligent curious traveller from England has no proper helps to guide him.'

The rest of the article is taken up with a guide to different parts of Scotland. This may have encouraged Edward Topham to come to Scotland, if he ever read the magazine

As few people in those days travelled about Scotland there was little need for good roads and hotels. In England and France, where more travelling was done, the inns were usually clean and comfortable. But not in Scotland. Even in Edinburgh the inns were bad. A pile of straw on the stone floor was all that many a weary traveller had for a bed. The food was coarse and the service was poor, with inn-keepers who were dirty and slovenly. But the complaints of travellers like Edward Topham must have done some good, for some years later, another English visitor wrote: 'No country has handsomer or better inns than Scotland. . . . I have the highest *commendation* to bestow on the civility of the Scottish inn-keepers.' So you see inns improved as more tourists came to Scotland. Edinburgh had several hotels within a few years after Edward Topham's visit. In the meantime, however, you can imagine how he felt after his journey from Newcastle, along roads that made travelling difficult except on horseback. Fortunately he found better lodgings in a house in the main street of Edinburgh. Little did he think then that after six months he would be sorry to leave the city. Perhaps we can understand why when we know more about Edinburgh and its people.

2 Edinburgh in 1774

From his lodgings in the High Street of Edinburgh, opposite the Mercat Cross to be exact, Edward Topham was well placed for touring the town. Perhaps he set out early next morning. At the front of the book is a map of the city that was drawn about this time. You will find it useful to locate the streets and buildings you read about. Possibly he made first for the Castle, the oldest part of the city and round which it had grown. He would walk up the High Street, which was part of a longer street that ran from the Castle to the royal palace of Holyroodhouse, called the Royal Mile.

The Castle had many interesting things to see. High up was the little chapel used by Saint Margaret of Scotland, that Saxon princess who fled from England at the time of the Norman Conquest, and married the Scottish king, Malcolm Canmore. Edward Topham might have been shown the royal

Edinburgh Castle seen from the Grassmarket

apartments, where much later than the time of St. Margaret, Mary Queen of Scots gave birth to James VI of Scotland who became the first king of both Scotland and England. In Topham's day the Castle was used as barracks for about a thousand soldiers, who could be seen drilling and standing about beside the great cannon that still peeped out through the thick walls overlooking the city 400 feet below.

Strong though the Castle was, it did not stop English invaders in the Middle Ages from burning the city down more than once. To protect themselves the inhabitants built a wall round their town, which, you will see from the map, was still standing in Edward Topham's time. Notice that it goes only part of the way round the centre of the town. The north side was protected by a deep moat called the Nor' Loch, and the steep-sided castle rock guarded its west side. All along the wall you will see marked several 'ports'. These were the gateways into the city, which till recently had been closed every night. The wall itself was no longer needed for protecting the city

Old houses in the West Port

5

from attackers. In fact, as the map shows, many people now lived outside the walls. Shortly after this time the walls were cleared away to make space for more houses and streets.

Edinburgh was a very crowded city. As Edward Topham told a friend: 'The High Street in Edinburgh is inhabited by a greater number of persons than in any street in Europe.' People had built their houses close together for safety inside the walls, but they used up all the room available and so, as more people came to live in the town, they had to build upwards, adding more and more floors to the houses as they were needed. Off the High Street were many *wynds*, *closes* and

College Wynd

entries. Edward Topham learned that a wynd was what he would call a lane, and a close was an alley. Of these side streets he wrote:

'They are many of them so very steep that it requires great attention to the feet to prevent falling; but so well accustomed are the Scotch to that position of the body required in descending these *declivities,* that I have seen a Scotch girl run down them with great swiftness in *pattens.*'

They were sometimes called after a former landowner, for example Halkerston's Wynd, Borthwick's Close and Geddes' Entry; or else they were known by a local landmark; such as Fleshmarket Close and Playhouse Close.

From the Castle Edward Topham would walk down the Lawnmarket and come upon the important buildings of Edinburgh—the Tolbooth, Parliament Hall, St Giles Cathedral and the Royal Exchange—all near one another. The

The Tolbooth and St. Giles's Cathedral

Tolbooth was a very old building, dark and gloomy both out- and in, and so tall that it shut out the light from the houses beside it. It was now only the town jail, but at one time the town council, the law courts and Parliament had all met here too. People called it the 'Heart of Midlothian'. Close by was

Parliament Hall, where the Scottish parliament had met in the years just before the Union of the Parliaments of Scotland and England. Since 1707 it had been taken over by the Court of Session and the High Court of Justiciary, the chief law courts of Scotland. Alongside the Tolbooth rose the historic St. Giles' Cathedral, where four separate congregations could hold their service under one roof. The famous John Knox had been minister here at the time of the Reformation two hundred years earlier. Beside the old church had stood the Mercat Cross until it was taken away in 1756 when the High Street was being made wider. It was still a favourite meeting-place.

The Royal Exchange

Merchants still preferred to do business here as they had done for centuries in the open air, instead of in the impressive Royal Exchange that was built opposite for them in 1761. Eventually the Town Council took it over for their meetings.

Like many other visitors to Edinburgh Mr Topham was

impressed with the High Street as he shows in one of his letters: 'You have seen the famous street at Lille in France, la rue Royale, which is said to be the finest in Europe; but which I assure you, is not to be compared either in length or breadth to the High Street at Edinburgh.'

Looking up the High Street

He was particularly pleased to find that he could keep his shoes clean because the town was so well paved. He wrote to his friend: 'The pavement of the whole town is excellent; the granite is dug from the hills close to the town, and brought at very small expense. They finish it with an exactness which the London workmen are indifferent about.'

At the foot of the High Street Edinburgh ended and another town began—the Canongate, with its own parish church and Tolbooth. It got this name because it was a burgh that had grown up in the Middle Ages beside the abbey of Holyrood, which was built in the eleventh century on land granted by

9

King David I to the monks. By the eighteenth century the houses in Edinburgh and the Canongate were no longer separate towns, although the Canongate, as you will see from the map, lay outside the walls of Edinburgh.

Study the map more closely and you will see that the Canon-

Moray House in the Canongate

gate houses are not so tightly packed together as those farther up the Royal Mile. Many of the town houses of lords and ladies were here. They faced each other across the street with gardens behind. An Edinburgh gentleman estimated that shortly before this, in 1769 to be precise, there lived in this area,

2	dukes	7	*lords of session*
16	earls	13	baronets
2	countesses	4	commanders-in-chief
7	lords	2	'eminent men'

At the foot of the Canongate Edward Topham found himself in the grounds of the Palace of Holyroodhouse and the Abbey of Holyrood. Perhaps Edward Topham was a little disappointed by what he saw. The beautiful old abbey was a neglected ruin and the Palace was deserted. Kings and queens had lived in it until 1603 when King James VI went off to

Holyrood Abbey and the Palace

London to rule both England and Scotland. It was an ancestor of his, James IV, who had built the Palace a hundred years before to welcome from England his young bride, Margaret, Henry VII's daughter. The famous Mary Queen of Scots spent most of her stay in Scotland here; this was where her secretary, David Rizzio, was murdered before her eyes. After 1603 when kings spent all their time in England there was little need for this royal palace and it was allowed to fall into disrepair until Charles II ordered it to be modernised and enlarged. His brother spent a few years in it, then it lay empty again till 1745, when Prince Charles Edward Stewart, better known as 'Bonnie Prince Charlie', made it his headquarters for six weeks during the Jacobite Rebellion. In Edward Topham's time it was empty again. The royal family never came here to stay.

After looking up at the great hill within the grounds of the Palace, Arthur's Seat, which had been used as a quarry for Edinburgh houses for hundreds of years, Edward Topham would possibly make his way back to the centre of the town by the Cowgate, the road that ran parallel to the Royal Mile. This contained some elegant old houses, which, though now shabby and *dilapidated*, had once been the residences of Scottish noblemen and foreign ambassadors. During his visit he attended a concert here in St Cecilia's Hall copied from an Italian opera house.

From the Cowgate Edward Topham might have been guided up one wynd to the High School of Edinburgh and another to the Infirmary. When he called on the professors at the 'Town's College' as the University was called, he probably went up the narrow College Wynd. From here it would not take him long to reach Heriot's Hospital, a large building in

Heriot's Hospital

the shape of a *quadrangle* standing in its own grounds on high ground south of the Castle. This was not a hospital in the modern sense, but, like the High School, a school for boys. Many visitors thought this building looked more like a royal palace than Holyrood did.

The Cowgate, as you will see, opens out on to a long open space called the Grassmarket. This was where farmers bought and sold their produce. It was also where public executions often took place, as Edward Topham saw for himself

The road to the west and north ran out from the Grass-market. It passed through a cluster of houses at the West Port which had once been part of a little burgh on its own, called Portsburgh, but which was now one of the many *suburbs* of Edinburgh. New parts were being added to the city around this time, first on the south side and then to the north. On the south side the houses were arranged like English ones in squares. The most famous was George Square, which was still being built during Edward Topham's visit. The houses were larger and more comfortable than those in the Royal Mile. They were healthier too out here in the country. With

George Square

other streets going up nearby, this was growing into a very select neighbourhood. With the Meadows close by for strolling in, there were pleasant walks, where not so long before there had been the marshy ground known as the Burgh Loch.

Meanwhile over to the north of the city on fields that stretched down to the sea, the Town Council was planning a whole new town. The man responsible for this bold *project* was George Drummond, seven times elected to be Lord Provost of Edinburgh. He had also built other improvements in the town, such as the Infirmary and the Royal Exchange. In the 1760s, after years of talking, the scheme for the New Town actually went ahead. An Act of Parliament gave the town council power to extend the bounds of the city. Then the Nor' Loch was drained, a bridge across it was started and a competition was arranged to find the best design for the proposed New Town. The winner of the contest was a young architect called James Craig. This is what his plan looked like.

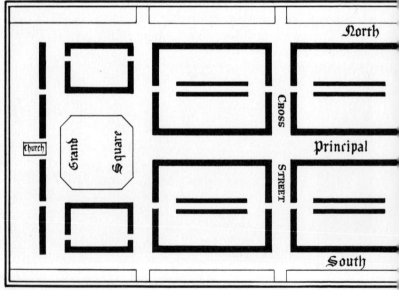

James Craig's

It is a perfectly simple plan to us in the twentieth century, but in the eighteenth it was quite new to the people of Edinburgh. This is how it was described:

'It has three streets almost a mile in length, running from east to west, *intersected* with cross-streets at proper distances. The most northerly, called Queen Street, is 100 feet broad, and commands an extensive *prospect* of the Forth, the county of Fife, and the shipping on the river. That called George Street, which is in the middle, is no less than 115 feet wide. It is *terminated* at each end by two very elegant and *extensive* squares; that on the east end is called St Andrew Square, the other, not yet finished, Charlotte Square. Princes Street is the most southerly, and extends from the northern *extremity* of the bridge quite to the west end of the town.'

In one of his letters Edward Topham wrote about it:

'The New Town has been built upon one *uniform* plan, which is the only means of making a city beautiful. Great

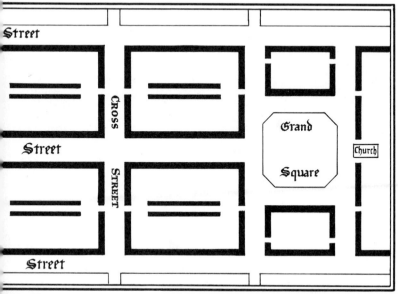

The New Town

15

parts of this plan as yet remain to be executed, though they proceed as fast as their supplies of money will allow them. . . . In no town that I ever saw, can such a contrast be found *betwixt* the ancient and modern architecture, or anything that better merits the observation of a stranger.' In October 1767 the first house in the New Town was started. Then, slowly at first but steadily, the plan took shape until by about 1800 it was complete. By then more houses were needed and so more went up.

All this was after Edward Topham's time. He saw the New Town only in its early stages when many people were shaking their heads and saying that no good would come from these changes and that nothing would persuade them to move from the Old Town, their own 'Auld Reekie', so called because of the 'reek' or smoke from its many chimneys.

3 Edinburgh Folk

In 1755 it was estimated that Edinburgh had 57,195 inhabitants and in 1791 this figure had risen to 81,865. Twenty years later the population had risen further to 103,143. By this time, however, Edinburgh had slipped from its place as second largest city in Britain. London was still first with two million inhabitants and Glasgow was now second with 100,090. These last figures are more accurate than earlier ones because people were now being counted regularly in a census every ten years. The first one in Britain was taken in 1801.

What kinds of jobs did all these people in Edinburgh work at? We can get some idea from the city's street directories, the first of which appeared in 1774. In this one the citizens are listed according to their social rank as follows:

Lords of Session
Advocates
Writers to the Signet
Solicitors
Clerks
Physicians
Noblemen and Gentlemen
Merchants
Grocers
Shipmasters
Surgeons
Brewers
School and Writing Masters
Milliners
Room-setters

Although the list does not include everybody (many people refused to be included) it shows who were considered the most important people in town. The first five groups of people were lawyers who were usually to be found in and around Parliament Hall.

They were all fairly comfortably off. Judges were paid a salary of about £500, a princely sum in those days. Advocates and solicitors charged fees according to the kind of business they carried out and how much their clients could afford. They had always plenty of work, buying and selling property, making wills and settling disputes between clients in and out of court.

Other well-to-do people were ministers of city churches and university professors with salaries of about £120. Merchants were even wealthier with profits from the goods they sold.

At the same time, a skilled tradesman such as a carpenter, took home wages of 1s 10d a day, while a maidservant got 30s a half-year and a book-seller's apprentice got 4s a week. The cost of living was going up and so were wages, though not so quickly as prices.

Some people did not seem to work at all—the 'Noblemen and Gentlemen' of the list in the street directory. These were landowners, or 'lairds', who lived on the rents from tenants on their country estates. Many of them were becoming quite rich from the improvements they were making on their farms to produce more crops and livestock. Such farmers were known as the 'Improvers'.

The street directory makes little mention of the city's many industries. Brewers are listed, however. Their industry was long established because of the excellent spring water found in the Canongate. Beer was made in Leith also, and so was glass for bottles. Most people there, however, worked at jobs to do with the sea. Along the Water of Leith many mills made linen, snuff, and especially paper. Books were published and printed in the city for the lawyers, university students and pupils at school.

Edinburgh, however, was not an industrial city of factories

as Glasgow and Birmingham were becoming at this time of the Industrial Revolution. It was a city of small workshops with skilled craftsmen producing gold and silver ware, furniture and carriages that were shipped even to Paris and Russia. The building of the New Town brought more work to others such as masons, builders, carpenters and plasterers.

Sometimes there was no work at all for many people and they had to go to the Poor House. In 1778 there were over 400 men and about 180 women there, some of whom were too old to work. Those who could were allowed to keep twopence out of every shilling they earned.

Then there were the town beggars. Only those with the town's badge were allowed to beg and the others were sent back to their own town or village. Some preferred begging to living in the Poor House.

Before the New Town was built Edinburgh was such a crowded place that everybody knew one another. Highborn and low, rich and poor they all spoke the old Scots tongue.

A Beggar's Badge

Since people from the south of England found this language hard to follow many Scotsmen had to learn to speak English when they went to work in England. Edward Topham remarked that Scottish people 'write English as a foreign language though Edinburgh society *manifest* an anxiety to rid themselves of a Scots accent'. Some even took lessons from men who claimed to be teachers of English. One of these was an actor who gave lectures to about three hundred gentlemen who practised what he told them without realising that their English teacher was an Irishman who spoke with a strong

Irish accent!

There were quite a few people in Edinburgh whose native language was neither Scots nor English. These were the Gaelic-speaking Highlanders. Many of the women were maid-

One of the Cadies

servants (many families could afford at least one) and the men were police-men of the City Guard or chair-men. When they were not paid enough for carrying a passenger in a *sedan chair*, they used to swear at him knowing that he would not understand one word they were saying.

Many Highlanders worked as cadies (pronounced 'cawdies'). a most useful set of men, as Edward Topham found out:

'These are a society of men who constantly attend the Cross in the High Street, and whose *office* it is to do anything anybody may want and discharge any kind of business. Whether you stand in need of a valet, a thief-catcher or a bully, your best resource is the *fraternity* of cadies. In short they are the guard-ians of the city, and there are fewer robberies and less housebreaking in Edinburgh than anywhere else.'

Truly there was a rich variety of people who called themselves Edinburgh folk.

4 At Home in the Old Town

When strangers came to town looking for a friend's house they usually asked the way from a cadie. Cadies knew where everybody lived, which was just as well, for not until 1782 did the streets have name-plates and house-numbers. In the street directory people were located like this:

Mrs Greig, teacher of English, Castlehill

Mrs Richardson, gentlewoman, Cowgate foot

Mrs Ramsay, makes grave-clothes, Cowgate head

William Johnstone, grocer, head of Baxter's Close.

John Allan, barber, Grassmarket, north side

Let us imagine that you are a visitor to the Old Town of Edinburgh in the eighteenth century. The houses are all made of stone, brought from the many quarries in and around the town. The roofs are covered with red *pantiles*, though some of the little cottages on the outskirts of the town have roofs of thatch.

The most famous Edinburgh houses are in the Lawnmarket and High Street. Visitors gaze at them, counting the flats of the tall tenements, wondering how it can possibly be safe to live at such a height. Nowhere else in Britain are houses so tall. Here is Edward Topham's description of them:

'The style of building here is much like the French. The houses, however, in general, are higher, as some rise to twelve and one in particular to thirteen storeys in height. But to the front of the street nine or ten storeys is the common run; it is the back part of the *edifice* which, by being built on the slope of a hill, sinks to that amazing depth, so as to form the above number. The buildings are divided by extremely thick partition walls, into large houses, which are here called 'lands', and each storey of a land is called a house.'

Houses in the Old Town: Gladstone's Land in the Lawnmarket

To reach your friend's house you turn off the High Street down a wynd so narrow that neighbours in the top storeys can lean out and shake hands across it. You have to climb up a steep staircase inside a tower the height of the houses. The stair is very dark and narrow and perhaps dirty too. You can count on meeting almost anyone here, because people of all ranks live together under the same roof. You can expect to collide with a countess or trip over a cadie. Down in the basement and up in the garrets live the chimney sweeps and labourers in

Down a Close

single-ends that cost about 18s a year in rent. Better-off people live in between —noblemen and lawyers, merchants, ministers and doctors. A nobleman might have a flat of six rooms—sitting-room, dining-room, three bedrooms, with a kitchen as well, and pay £20 as rent for a year.

Reaching your friend's flat you pull up and down the little ring that is attached to the notched piece of iron, the 'risp' or 'tirlin' pin' on the door. Bells and knockers are not yet in use. A maidservant with bare feet opens the door and invites you to come into the *parlour*, by way of a narrow, dimly lit hall. Your friend bids you welcome and

A risp or tirlin' pin

then shows you round his house.

There are sash windows about two feet square and made up of several small panes. They have no curtains but wooden shutters are drawn across instead. All the rooms are quite small with low ceilings. These have elaborate designs worked in the plaster, but some poor tenants have no plaster ceilings at all, only bare pinewood planks laid across the beams, still full of cracks and holes, which serve both as their ceiling and the floor of the flat above. The walls are decorated in various ways. Some people prefer wooden panelling to the plain white plaster, even when it has designs painted on it: flowers and landscapes in the parlour and bunches of fruit in the dining-room. Perhaps your friend may be thinking of decorating his best rooms with the recently invented wallpaper. The floors are made of polished timber that his maidservant keeps shiny with oil and pitch. At least she does not have many rugs and carpets to keep clean. Down in the cellars and in the first floor flat, the floors are made of stone and housewives scrub them with sand.

Poor tenants furnish their one room with a deal table, a wooden chair or two and several stools, a dresser, an *aumry* and a 'kist' or chest for storing linen. The bed fits into a recess in the wall and is hidden by a curtain. Your friend, being better off, has almost too much furniture. Most of it is made of mahogany, walnut or chestnut. Some comes from the Netherlands and England. The most fashionable furniture is made in the workrooms of the famous cabinet-makers, Chippendale, Sheraton and Hepplewhite. It is very light and graceful. The long dining-room table has chairs to match and a tall cabinet displays the dishes of silver, pewter and china. The parlour is sometimes called the 'lady's room'. It contains leather-covered easy chairs as well as cane-bottomed ones. There is also a *spinet* and an *escritoire* and, essential in Edinburgh with its cold winds in winter whirling up the stairs, a tall screen for keeping

24

Furniture of the Time

A cruisie lamp

out draughts. This room has at least one bed too, either in the middle of the room or behind the door. Space is limited and so beds are put up everywhere and servants sleep on the floor. Wardrobes, chests of drawers and grandfather clocks may stand in the hall.

People burn coal in open fireplaces. Some of them are decorated with brass ornaments and white and blue Dutch tiles. At night candles or little oil lamps called 'cruisies' are lit.

Our friend has no lavatory or bathroom in his house. There is no running water in any of the houses. All water has to be brought up in jugs and *pitchers* from the public wells in the street below. Instead

25

of a lavatory there are chamber pots which are emptied out of the window into the street. The Town Council has forbidden this, but at ten o'clock you can hear the shouts of 'Gardyloo!' (from the French 'prenez garde a l'eau'), which is a warning to passers-by to stand clear. Next morning—except Sunday—the streets are cleaned. The smell of the Edinburgh streets on Sunday is said to be the origin of the expression 'the flowers of Edinburgh', which is the name of a well-known country dance!

Most people in Edinburgh are quite content to live in this kind of house. It has many drawbacks, however, and so, as the New Town houses go up people start to move out of the Old Town.

5 In the New Town

Leaving a house in the Old Town for one in the New Town was like going to a strange new world. At first few wanted to go. As Edward Topham tells us: 'One old lady fancies she should be lost, another that she should be blown away in going over the new bridge; and a third lives in the old style, because she is sure that these new fashions can come to "nae guid".' The collapse of the North Bridge did not help to encourage people.

Then the Town Council decided to coax people to move by offering £20 to the first person who would live in the New Town. The first house in the New Town was in Thistle Court. The man who bought the first house in Princes Street was more fortunate still: he was allowed to live there without paying rates. From then on the New Town began to grow.

Houses in the New Town: Queen Street

Imagine now that our friend has removed from the Old Town and has invited us to look round his house in the New Town.

This is a 'house to itself', not a block of flats. It has three floors, an attic and a basement below street level. Along the front of the house runs an iron railing. The main door has an elegant *portico* and the window above the doorway has panes of glass shaped like a fan or a flower.

We look around us while we wait for an answer to our ring at the bell. We see the steep little stair for tradesmen and servants that leads from the street down to the basement below. The neighbouring houses which join on to this one are all the same height. The Town Council will not allow people to build them higher than three storeys. Most of them are made of honey-coloured sandstone, which looks very fresh and clean. Those at the eastern end are plainer than the ones farther west, some of which have decorated fronts and bow windows.

Splendid houses in Charlotte Square

The north side of Charlotte Square has the most splendid houses of all. You can see how the whole length of the street has been designed as if it were the front of one big house.

The maidservant invites us into a large hallway well lit from the skylight in the roof. Doors open off on both sides to a dining-room and a study, where our friend receives us. He shows us round his house, leading the way up the broad stone staircase, pointing out to us the decorated iron balustrade, and showing us through the drawing-rooms, bedrooms and little dressing-rooms on the two floors above. Upstairs in the attic are smaller rooms with low *coom-ceilings* and tiny windows, the nursery where the children play.

The main rooms of the house are very spacious and full of light coming through tall windows, each with its twelve small panes of glass. At night, when the shutters are closed and the curtains drawn, they are still bright with candle-light from the crystal *chandeliers*. The ceilings are high and covered with intri-

A New Town Ceiling

cate designs worked in plaster, that are repeated in the *cornice* and round the walls. Delicate shades of blue and green are used as well as white. Some houses have walls covered with plain wallpaper instead. Family portraits and paintings of country scenes in heavy gilt frames line the walls. The window curtains are made of brocade or rich velvet. Rugs and carpets cover the polished wooden floors. Fireplaces are made of marble or wood covered with stucco to tone in with the room

A New Town Fireplace

Tables, chairs and long couches with slim legs and sometimes painted white and gold, are made to match also. The study has a great desk and leather easy-chairs and is lined with tall book-cases. There are many rooms: beds are kept in the bedrooms in this house! There are two drawing-rooms and one room can be used for receiving guests in the morning (a morning-room), and another as a music room. But thought this is one of the most splendid and up-to-date houses in Britain around 1800, it has neither bathroom nor lavatory. Only later were these made out of small rooms and large cupboards under the stairs.

Keeping such a large house warm and clean is not easy, and thus many servants are needed. They live in the basement and their long day's work begins before six o'clock. It is always half-light here but at least there is running water in the kitchen. Water still has to be heated in a pot or kettle over the great kitchen range. There is ample storage space: linen cupboards, pantries with stone shelves for keeping food fresh, and a wine cellar. There is a laundry in the basement too; the maids take the washing out to bleach in the sun in the Queen Street gardens or on the slopes of the Calton Hill. Coal for the fires is dropped through a manhole in the pavement into the coal cellar underneath.

Not all the servants live inside the house. The coachman has a little house above the stables at the foot of the garden behind the house. Its windows look out on to the narrow cobbled *mews* lane that runs between the main streets.

Of course only the very rich people of Edinburgh can afford to live in a house like this. In the 1770s a house in St Andrew Square costs nearly £2,000, and some are twice as dear. It costs about £100 a year to rent one. There are cheaper houses in the New Town: small flats in narrow side streets, such as Rose Street and Thistle Street, where the tradesmen and shop-keepers live.

Unlike twentieth-century new towns this one had no factories, shops or offices. Apart from the Assembly Rooms, the Physicians' Hall and two churches there was nothing but houses. It was a residential suburb. In a very short time, however, many of the houses were converted into shops, offices, banks and hotels; by the 1820s Princes Street was lined with them. Instead of George Street, Princes Street was the most important street of the New Town and the main street of Edinburgh.

Living in the New Town had its disadvantages. People missed the friendliness of the Old Town. Here they could easily feel cut off from their friends. They complained of the cold east winds and the gusts from the north that blew off their hats and forced them to clutch at the railings for support in the wide open streets. The High Street was a long way off; elderly lawyers and businessmen were quite out of breath from the climb up to it. But this did not prevent them from being proud of their houses with their open views over the gardens to the north and south.

After the New Town was completed the city went on expanding to the north and west towards the Water of Leith, eastwards around the Calton Hill and southwards also. In a city like Edinburgh, with its many hills and valleys, bridges were needed to link up the different parts. The North Bridge was completed, then over the Cowgate the South Bridge and George IV Bridge, Regent Bridge from Princes Street to the Calton Hill and leading westwards over the Water of Leith and the Dean Village towards Queensferry, the Dean Bridge. There was still a need to link the New Town directly with the High Street, so with earth from the foundations of houses in the New Town, the Mound was created across the drained Nor' Loch.

New public buildings went up too. Register House was built at the foot of the North Bridge for keeping important documents. Opposite, in what was then called Shakespeare Square, was the Theatre Royal. New buildings were put up for the University and the High School, and an observatory on the Calton Hill.

To make way for some of these new buildings old ones had to come down. Some fell during the great fires in the centre of the Old Town in the 1820s. Others were pulled down deliberately. One that was much missed was the old Tolbooth, the 'Heart of Midlothian'.

Many older citizens thought that the changes were a mixed blessing. One of these was William Creech, a publisher, whose 'Fugitive Pieces' contain references to them; for example, he notes:

'In 1763—people of quality and fashion lived in houses which, in 1783 are inhabited by tradesmen and people in humble and ordinary life. The *Lord Justice-Clerk* Tinwald's house was lately possessed by a French teacher—*Lord President* Craigie's house is at present possessed by a rouping-wife or saleswoman of old furniture—and Lord Drummore's house was lately left by a chairman for want of accommodation. . . . The great Marquis of Argyle's house in the Castlehill, is possessed by a hosier at £12 per annum.'

And so he goes on to other examples. It is plain to see what was happening to the Old Town. Only the poor people were left. Many of them could not afford the money or were not interested in preserving the old houses, which soon fell into ruin. The Old Town was allowed to become a vast slum—dirty, rat-infested and thoroughly unsafe. The people in the New Town had lost interest in their old one.

6 Eating and Drinking

When English visitors came to Scotland in the eighteenth century nothing reminded them more that they were in a different country than the food the people ate. The names of many dishes had to be translated. Howtowdie, they learnt, was a pullet boiled in rich gravy with eggs; Cabbieclaw was boiled cod in egg sauce; Cock-a-leekie, a chicken soup with leeks; and Powsowdie, sheep's head broth. There were also Haggis, to Scotsmen a delicious meal, but to some strangers horrible. Cuts of meat were different, and so were the measures Scottish cooks used, for example:

Scots	English
1 mutchkin =	1 pint
1 pint	= 2 quarts
1 quart	= 1 gallon

Some words used in the kitchen were strange too, though possibly not to French people, as these examples show:

Scots	French	English
ashet	assiette	dish for serving meat
jiggot	gigot	leg of mutton
tassie	tasse	cup

What English visitors loved were the fifty-odd kinds of tea-bread, marmalade, the many kinds of sweets and, by the beginning of the nineteenth century, whisky. This drink, made in the Highlands, was just becoming popular in the Lowlands.

Food was generally plentiful in Edinburgh, except in war-time and when the harvest was poor. Prices were not too high. Here are some that an English traveller noted in 1771:

Beef, from 5d to 3½d per lb
Mutton, from 4d to 3½d per lb
Bacon, 7d per lb
Chickens, per pair, 8d to 1s

Pigeons, per dozen, from 8*d* to 5*s*

Butter, in summer, 8*d*; in winter, 1*s* per lb

Large turkey, 4*s* or 5*s*.

Much of the food was supplied locally. Wheat, oats and barley for flour and beer came from the fertile farms of the Lothians. Cattle were brought for slaughter from the Highlands. Milkmaids on horseback sold milk and 'soordook', or buttermilk. Fishwives from Newhaven and Fisherrow, with creels on their backs, brought in the haddock, cod and herring which their menfolk had caught in the North Sea. From the Firth of Forth came delicious oysters and crabs that were the delight of Edinburgh supper parties. There were fresh green vegetables and soft fruits from around Musselburgh, and through the port of Leith arrived lemons from Italy, oranges, almonds and figs from Spain, chestnuts and wine from France, and rice, rum and sugar from America.

A Newhaven Fishwife with her creel

The city had also plenty of clean, sparkling water brought from springs at Swanston out near the Pentland Hills in underground iron pipes to a reservoir on the Castle Hill. From here it was led to public wells down the length of the Royal Mile. Water cadies, men and women in duffle-coats, carried the splashing buckets up the narrow stairs to customers in the Old Town. In the New Town water came with turning the tap in the kitchen.

A Water Cadie at a Public Well

What do you think of this description of a grocer's shop?
'The windows exhibited quantities of sugar in different
varieties of brownness, hovering over which were swarms of
flies, in a state of frantic enjoyment. Sticks of black liquo-
rice leaned coaxingly on the second row of panes, flanked
by the tall glass jars of sweeties and peppermint drops;
behind these outward attractions, there were observable
yellow-painted barrels of whisky, rows of bottles of *porter*,
piles of cheeses of various complexions, *firkins* of salt
butter, and boxes of soap. At the counter were a number of
women and children buying articles, such as quarter-
ounces of tea and ounces of sugar; and the floor was
battered with dirt and *debris*.'

There were many shops like this one in the basements of the Old Town, small dark and dingy, with sacks of flour and large chests of tea, the home of rats and mice. Outside, the goods were advertised by signs painted in colour on the walls of the houses.

For butcher's meat, fruit and vegetables housewives went to the open-air markets in or near the High Street. Customers in the New Town went to their own market at Stockbridge. Neither in the market nor anywhere else was food sold ready wrapped, so shoppers had to bring their own jugs or baskets.

There were also many street vendors, shouting what they had for sale at the top of their voices in a kind of song. Fish-wives, for instance, sang out to advertise their fresh oysters in a rising scale: 'Caller ou-ou-ou-ou!' Other hawkers shouted, 'Wall cresses!' 'Curds and green whey!' and 'Peas and beans, hot and warm!' Other vendors sold brushes, sand and coal.

Cooking took up a lot of the housewife's time. There were no pre-cooked foods in tins or packets. All her cooking was done on the open hearth till ranges made at the Carron Iron Works near Falkirk were installed late in the eighteenth century. Not every kitchen had even a brick oven for making bread. Bannocks and oatcakes were baked on a large round girdle or sometimes on a flat stone in front of the fire. Pots were made of heavy iron; some housewives managed with only one for their stews, soups, sauces and heating water for washing up. When the price of tea fell in the 1790s copper kettles began to appear in kitchens, and they were polished till they shone.

A Girdle for Oatcakes and Scones

37

Meal-times got later throughout the century. In 1760 breakfast was at seven or eight, dinner between one and two and supper about seven o'clock. In between there was time for refreshments, in mid-morning—the 'meridian' or the 'twal' hours', when brandy or weak ale was drunk, and the 'four hours' in the afternoon. Claret was drunk at first, then tea. This was the time when Edinburgh ladies used to gather for little parties in one another's houses in the Old Town, sitting on the bed for a sofa, with their teaspoons numbered to save confusion between servings of tea, and passing round the biscuits. By the end of the century, when gentlefolks were having suppers after nine, lesser people were still having their meals at the old times, the old-fashioned among the men still keeping on their bonnets when they ate. Even then no one would dream of starting a meal until grace was said. Here is a grace, the Covenanter's, nowadays call the 'Selkirk' Grace:

> Some hae meat that canna eat,
> And some wad eat that want it;
> But we hae meat, and we can eat,
> And sae the Lord be thankit.

With their wooden bowls and horn spoons, the poorest had little to eat but oatmeal. It appeared at breakfast as porridge.

Wooden Bowls and Horn Spoon

In the middle of the day it was added to a rich vegetable soup called kail, and made into bannocks that were eaten with a little fish, meat or chicken. The fish was very often herring, cooked in oatmeal. At the end of the day there was often a light pudding made from oatmeal and called 'sowans'. Gradually potatoes replaced bannocks at dinner and wooden plates were replaced by dishes of pewter and *delft*.

The better-off people could afford to eat off china plates and the very rich—on special occasions—off silver. Their food was more varied, with more meat and less oatmeal. We can tell this from the many cookery-books that now began to appear. They are full of recipes for rich, tempting dishes; some of them are quite simple and call for ordinary everyday materials, though requiring great quantities of eggs, butter and cream; others demand many spices and herbs and also such things as rose-petals, nettles and marigolds!

For the rich, breakfast was a large meal. Mutton, beef or chicken and a tankard of ale to follow were quite common, till the English breakfast became fashionable, with its toast, marmalade and tea or coffee. Dinner consisted of barley broth, beef—often minced *collops*—boiled fowls or fish of various kinds prepared in many different ways. Last of all came delicious-sounding sweets such as *flummery* or *syllabub*, or a *posset*. Here is a recipe for a syllabub from a cookery book that dates back to 1769:

WHIPT SILLABUBS
Cream, white wine, lemon, sugar.
Take a *mutchkin* of thick cream, put to it half a mutchkin of white wine, the juice of a lemon, and grate the rind in it; sweeten it to your taste, whisk it well, skim off the top as you are whisking it, and put it on a sieve; then put wine in the glass, either white or red, and a little sugar; then send it to table with teaspoons about it.

Sometimes a dish was served that was half-sweet and half-savoury, such as potatoes or eggs with stewed pears, or soup that had prunes in it. Turnips at first were treated as a sweet and vegetables were almost always put in soups instead of being served fresh. White bread was a delicacy for the gentry and eaten like cake. All dishes—soups, meats and sweets—appeared on the table at one serving until after 1800, when the English custom of serving them as separate courses was introduced.

Everyone drank heavily. Wines and spirits were very cheap, tea and coffee were expensive, milk could not be kept fresh for long and water was often dirty. The most popular drinks were ale, beer, brandy and claret, the favourite among the gentry till the war with France cut off supplies and made it an unpatriotic beverage, and port and sherry from Spain and Portugal took its place. At parties punch was a favourite drink, made from rum, sugar and lemons, and served hot. After the wars with France were over a new drink appeared at Edinburgh parties; champagne it was called.

7   The Clothes People Wore

Edinburgh's ladies and gentlemen were among the best dressed in the whole country, keeping up with the ever-changing fashions of London and Paris.

Clothes were then made mainly from linen and wool. Some of the cloth was woven in and around Edinburgh. Women still spun their own yarn, so there was hardly a house without its spinning-wheel. Some people still had their old hand looms for weaving, but power looms were taking over much of this work, especially over in the west. In the new mills, such as those at New Lanark on the River Clyde, cotton cloth was being made. It was finer than linen and wool, cheaper and more easily washed. Richer materials like velvet, satin and lace came from England, as did the best woollen cloth, which was smoother than Scottish cloth.

Men as well as women dressed in bright colours. At a ball men might wear suits of scarlet, light blue or green. All this changed in the nineteenth century when men's clothes were mostly black, grey and brown. All clothes—even men's shirts—had to be sewn by hand and made to measure. Most women could make clothes for themselves and their children. Even at the city's best private schools young ladies were taught dress-making, although there was no scarcity of clothiers in the city. According to the street directory for 1774 there were fifty-one tailors, eleven hatters, ten glove-makers, twenty-two milliners and thirty-five *mantua-makers*.

Portraits of the time show us how people dressed. On the next page is a lady in the height of fashion in 1775, in her long ball-gown of satin brocade or silk. It opens down the front to show the underdress, which sometimes is made of a different material in a contrasting colour. Notice how the overskirt is worn tucked up at the sides. Her underwear is made of linen or

A Lady of Fashion

flannel, and her stockings of wool. They come up to her knee and are supported by garters. She achieves the effect of a narrow waist by wearing tight-fitting stays and cane paniers for supporting her many petticoats. She carries a fan made of feathers. Her shoes are made of cloth to match her gown; they are not made for heavy wear, for she will travel by coach or sedan-chair. If it is wet she may wear iron pattens, and if it is very cold she can put on a heavy cloak with a hood and take a muff.

Ladies wear their hair very long. This one is dressed for a special occasion so she wears it piled up with woollen pads over a wire and gauze frame, greased, powdered and perfumed, and decorated with feathers and ribbons. She may wear a wig instead. When she returns her maid will put the wig on its stand.

A Lady's Shoe in a Patten

Most times a lady like this dresses quite simply in wool or cotton, with a light shawl over her shoulders crossed at the front, and her hair in ringlets under a cap or turban. Scottish ladies pride themselves on their good complexions; some clean their faces occasionally with milk, but they wear little make-up, only a little powder and rouge. A few old ladies can still be seen wearing patches on their face. This is a fashion from their young days.

This is how a humorous writer described a young lady of fashion in 1779:

Give Betsy a bushel of horsehair and wool,
    Of paste and *pomatum* a pound;
Ten yards of gay ribbon to deck her sweet skull,
    And gauze to encompass it round.
Of all the bright colours the rainbow displays,
    Are these ribbons which hang from her head,
And her flowers adapted to make the folk gay,
    For round the whole width are they spread.
Her flaps fly behind for a yard at the least,
    And her curls meet just under her chin;
And these curls are supported, to keep up the jest,
    With an hundred instead of one pin.
Her gown is tucked up to the hip on each side,

Shoes too high for a walk and a jump,
And to deck the sweet creature complete for a bride,
   The cork-cutter has made her a rump.
Thus finished in taste, while on her I gaze,
   I think I could take her for life;
But I fear to undress her, for out of her stays,
   I should find I had lost half my wife.

Lady with a Rump

This cartoon shows a woman wearing a dress with a 'rump' of cork, which was very fashionable at this time.

During the 1780s the fashions became simpler. The 'rump' or bustle having been removed, skirts hung in loose natural folds. Twenty years later dresses were simpler still, shorter and less full. The waist was high and the skirt reached only as far as the ankles without hoops or layers of petticoats. Lighter materials were now in demand, such as muslin, calico and gingham. Slippers were worn instead of high-heeled shoes. Out of doors, ladies dressed in short fur-lined jackets and boots. Hair styles were modelled on those of ancient Greece and Rome and so the hair was worn simply, swept back and tied in a knot at the back.

By the 1820s fuller styles were returning, as in this young lady's dress. The waist was back in its natural position, and ladies

A Lady of the 1820s

A Gentleman of the 1770s

were wearing tight stays, hoops and petticoats again. Skirts, however, were only ankle-length. Poke-bonnets, festooned with ribbons and feathers, framed ladies' faces, with their hair parted in the middle of rows of curls and dressed high at the back.

Men's fashions changed too. In the early 1770s a well-dressed young man looked like this. He is wearing a single-breasted frock-coat that reaches his knees. It has large deep pockets and sleeves with wide cuffs. The lapels of his coat fold back to show off his long waist-coat, possibly made of silk, and sometimes richly embroidered or gaily striped. It can button up to the neck though it is worn open to leave room for his cravat. This is made of linen and so is his shirt. Sometimes a shirt has rows of ruffles down the front and lace at the cuffs.

Knee breeches are made of different material from the coat. By the 1790s they are made of buckskin or *nankeen* and so tight that one writer described them 'as if sewed or pasted to the skin'. Stockings are made of wool, silk or cotton and come over the knee. White is fashionable, but they can be of assorted colours or striped. Gentlemen take great pride in their shapely calves; some men wear false ones made of cork! Shoes fasten with a buckle, but by the 1780s it is becoming smart to wear black

'as if sewed or pasted to the skin'

45

riding boots with a cut-away tail-coat even for town wear. In cold weather a man may put on a heavy riding cloak, and for walking about town he may carry an umbrella. This however is still a novelty; it was a curiosity in Edinburgh in the 1760s.

Every man, even the poorest, wears some kind of hat. Dark three-cornered hats, made of felt or velvet, are the most common, but towards the end of the century tall hats are being worn. Many gentlemen still wear wigs. It is said that a man's occupation can be judged by the kind he wears. Men have to have their heads shaved or their hair cut very short. Even then they are glad to take their wigs off at home and put on a cap or turban. Many young men wear their hair long and tie it at the back in a little tail with a ribbon. They usually dress it with hair-cream called pomatum and dust it with powder.

Gentlemen carry little snuff-boxes because most gentlemen and many ladies enjoy their pinches of snuff. And no gentleman would be properly dressed without his walking stick, gloves and large linen handkerchief.

A Gentleman of about 1830

By 1800 there were many changes in men's fashions. Wigs were going out of favour, except among lawyers. Men were wearing their hair short and natural, especially because there was a tax of a guinea a year for wearing hair-powder. High-crowned hats were taking the place of the three-cornered ones.

Shirt collars were appearing above the cravat and waistcoats were getting shorter. The greatest change seen in the introduction of trousers instead of breeches. By about 1830 a gentleman dressed in town as in the picture opposite. His frock-coat is close-fitting, his trousers are kept in shape with straps under the instep, and he is wearing a tile hat. His coat is probably black. The eighteenth century is a distant memory.

Young people were dressed to look like miniature adults; some young girls were even put into stays! There were some differences, however. Girls tended to wear looser-fitting styles. But when the tight-waisted fashions of the 1820s returned, young girls lost their freedom. They had to put on long frilly *pantaloons* to cover their legs which otherwise would have shown under the flouncing skirts.

Boys are very often shown in portraits wearing open-necked shirts. They were not expected to wear wigs and they seem to have had fairly long hair. This is how an Edinburgh writer described the clothes he wore as a schoolboy around 1800:

'Round black velvet hats, a shirt fastened at the neck by a black ribbon, and except on dress days, unruffled. A cloth waistcoat, rather large, with two rows of buttons and button-holes so that it could be buttoned on either side: a single-breasted jacket, which in due time got a tail and became a coat; brown corduroy breeches tied at the knee by a showy knot of brown cotton tape; worsted stockings in winter, blue cotton stockings in summer, and white cotton for dress; clumsy shoes, made to be used on either foot, brass or copper buckles. The coat and waistcoat were always of glaring colours such as bright blue, grass green, and scarlet. A scarlet waistcoat and a bright green coat were very tony.'

Working people's clothes were not so colourful and were made of rougher materials. Men's suits and women's frocks

47

Two Country People

were made of homespun wool; and trousers—which working men wore before the gentry copied them—were often made of corduroy. Underwear was usually of a kind of linen called harn.

Above are two country people. The man is wearing the usual blue woollen bonnet. The woman has on a close-fitting frock called a jupp with a neckerchief round her shoulders and a mob cap on her head. She is wearing shoes, but many women in Edinburgh as well as in the country went barefoot. On Sunday, however, they would *hirple* to church in shoes.

According to writers of this time, the working people were dressing better than ever before. *The Statistical Account* shows us this too. In a country parish just outside Edinburgh, for example, a ploughman was able in 1790 to go dressed to church in a coat of blue cloth (costing 5*s* 6*d* per yard), a velvet vest, corduroy breeches, stockings of white cotton, calf-skin shoes, a shirt that had ruffles at the breast and a white muslin-fringed cravat. This was a sign of great change, for he would never have been able to afford to dress like this earlier in the century.

8   Fun and Games

Boys and girls played at many games that are still popular today. They rolled their hoops up and down the High Street, and in the back closes they played skipping games, leapfrog and hopscotch. Nearby there was plenty of open space to run about and fly kites. Every boy and girl loved to be taken to the waxworks in Leith Walk, or to the Krames, those open booths alongside St Giles where all kinds of toys were sold. One great excitement was to watch the balloon flights of the famous Vincent Lunardi. He made several in Edinburgh: the first, in 1785, took him over the sea and landed him in Fife.

Most people spent their evenings at home. Reading was popular. Edinburgh had a circulating library before most cities in the country. Many read the novels of Henry Mackenzie, Tobias Smollett, Sir Walter Scott and John Galt. Others preferred more serious reading, periodicals such as 'The Scots Magazine', 'The Edinburgh Review' and 'The Quarterly Review', and the local newspapers: the 'Edinburgh Evening Courant', the 'Caledonian Mercury', 'The Scotsman' and the 'Edinburgh Advertiser' all of which came out twice or three times a week. Rich people played card games such as whist.

Dinner parties were often held with dancing afterwards. This is how a hostess described one she gave in her house in the Old Town:

'On Wednesday I gave a ball. How do you think I *contrived* to stretch out this house to hold twenty-two people, and had nine couples always dancing? Yet this is true: it is also true that we had a table covered with *diverse* eatables all the time, and that everybody ate when they were hungry and drank when they were dry, but nobody ever sat down . . . Our fiddler sat where the cupboard is

49

and they danced in the dining room; the table was shipped into the window, and we had plenty of room. It made the bairns all vastly happy.'

At parties young ladies were expected to sing, accompanied by a guitar or spinet. Two popular songs were 'Caller Herring' and 'Will ye no' come back again?', written by Lady Nairne.

Many, however, went out for their entertainment. They could meet their friends at a tavern in the town. Johnnie Dowie's, a small dark place that was famed for its suppers, was possibly the most popular of all. For a change, ladies and gentlemen might take a *hackney carriage* down to the oyster cellars in Leith to eat oysters and drink punch, brandy or porter, then dance reels till dawn. In summer—when it did not rain—they could stroll in Comely Gardens near Holyrood to the sound of music under lanterns in the trees.

There was plenty to watch in the High Street all year round, but in winter around five o'clock in the evening there was always a stir at the head of one of the closes when sedan chairs drew up and out stepped ladies and gentlemen in their best clothes. They were going to the weekly Assembly, the highlight of Edinburgh's social life. Tickets for this dance cost 2s 6d each. It was very formal and dignified. Everybody had to go with a partner. Ladies sat on one side of the tiny hall and gentlemen on the other. A lady directress acted as a kind of mistress of ceremonies, announcing the items on the programme and seeing that everybody behaved properly. They danced stately *minuets* and livelier Scottish *strathspeys* and reels. Music was provided by a small orchestra. At the interval the dancers retired upstairs for tea or coffee or the oranges the gentlemen brought for their partners. Dancing stopped promptly on the stroke of eleven from St Giles' and the lady directress sent them all home. So popular were these assemblies that Assembly Rooms had to be opened for people who had moved away from the Old Town: one near George Square

The Assembly Rooms, George Street

and a magnificent one in the New Town in George Street. But these were not like those in the crowded little room in the Old Town.

Theatre-going was popular too, though early in the eighteenth century it had been banned. Down in the Canongate there was a small Playhouse where plays were put on between recitals of music. Leading players from London came here. When the great Sarah Siddons was playing one of her great parts, she was so popular that the meetings of the General Assembly of the Church of Scotland had to be so arranged that ministers and elders could have time to go and see her. In Shakespeare Square a Theatre Royal was opened for patrons in the New Town, who paid a shilling for a seat in the upper gallery and three shillings for a box.

There was a Musical Society with an orchestra made up of French horns, kettledrums, flutes, clarinets and a harpsichord which performed on winter evenings in St Cecilia's Hall in the Cowgate. The programme included music by leading composers—Bach, Handel, Corelli and Haydn. Well-known singers came from Italy and Germany to sing Scottish songs and arias from operas. When people moved to the New Town, however, they gave up coming to the concerts, which were discontinued.

Gentlemen had a great number of clubs they could attend in the evenings. These had the most unusual names—the Spendthrift Club, the Black Wigs, the Odd Fellows and the Dirty Club—and some curious customs too. Members of the Odd Fellows wrote their names upside down. Many leading citizens were members of the Freemasons, who met in their lodges to practise their secret craft and join in good fellowship afterwards.

For outdoor amusements there were bowls in summer, ice-skating and *curling* in winter. Golf was a very old Scottish game but few people in England played it yet. Edward Topham was obviously interested in it and described it to his English friend who had never seen it played,

'The diversion which is peculiar to Scotland, and in which all ages find great pleasure, is golf. They play it with a small leathern ball and a piece of wood, flat on one side, in the shape of a small bat, which is fastened at the end of a stick three or four feet long, at right angles to it. The art consists in striking the ball with this instrument into a hole in the ground, in a smaller number of strokes than your adversary. It requires no great exertion and strength, and all ranks and ages play it.'

Edinburgh people played it on the links down by the sea at Leith. In July this is also where the Caledonian Hunt held their races. The Leith Races attracted everybody, some to bet on the horses, others to enjoy the many sideshows. Leith was also becoming popular for its sea-bathing. This new craze in the eighteenth century led many rich people to spend holidays by the sea in the villas they built at Portobello and at Trinity. All the year round there was no excuse for being bored in Edinburgh.

9 At School in Edinburgh

At a time when parents in Britain did not have to send their children to school many Scottish ones chose to do so. In every parish there was a school where the sons and daughters of the laird sat beside the children of his humblest labourer. There were a few of these schools in the villages near Edinburgh; at Cramond and at Liberton, for example. They were very small. They had only one teacher, a man who was called the 'dominie'—from the Latin 'dominus' a master. He taught the 'three R's'—reading, writing and arithmetic—and religious knowledge. He would teach Latin to boys called 'lads o' pairts' who were very clever and eager to go on to the University.

Boys in Edinburgh whose parents wanted them to attend the University went to the High School. It was famous

The High School of Edinburgh

throughout Scotland for its size and learning. Many of the five hundred boys came from different parts of Scotland or from England. Some of its masters were distinguished scholars. It stood on the east side of the University and was run by the Town Council who appointed the Rector, as the headmaster was called, and charged the boys fees amounting to about half-a-guinea a quarter. They started about the age of nine and spent five or six years at school. Having learned to read and write already, they spent the next five years learning Latin and in their last year some Greek. Latin was needed to understand the lectures at the University, where many of them went at the age of fourteen to study for a degree to become lawyers, ministers and doctors.

Girls were not sent to the University: the idea of women doctors, lawyers and ministers was quite unthinkable. There was no point in teaching girls Latin, so there was no high school for them. Some girls attended small private boarding-schools, where they were taught to become young ladies. Here is the account that was sent to the father of one such young lady for a term at an Edinburgh finishing-school. It shows what she was taught and how much it cost. Remember that the prices are quoted in old Scottish money, which was equivalent to a twelfth of English money, and that unmarried ladies and girls were referred to as 'Mrs' and not 'Miss'.

Accompt the Laird of Kilravock for his daughter, Mrs Margaret Rose for her board and education, to Elizabeth Stratoun—

Imprimis, one quarter board, from the 2d September to the 2d of Decr.,	£60	0	0
Item, Dancing, one quarter	14	10	0
Item, One quarter singing and playing and *virginals*	11	12	0
Item, One quarter at writing	06	0	0
Item, for five writing books	01	0	0

Item, for satin seam, and silk to her satin seam	06	0	0
Item, One set of wax-fruits	06	0	0
Item, One looking glass that she broke	04	16	0
Item, frame for a satin seam	01	10	0
Item, 12 dozen of linen for smocks to her at 12 shillings per *ell*	07	4	0
Item, One quarter at writing, which I paid before she entered as boarder, from the 2d December to 2d March	06	0	0
Item, a glass for her satin seam	01	4	0

Summa £125 16 0

Discharged by Elisabeth Stratoun, *indweller* in Edinburgh.

You would have picked out some children in Edinburgh by their clothes: girls in green and blue frocks and boys in light brown suits with leather caps. These were the pupils of the four hospitals or boarding-schools run by charitable foundations, two for girls—the Merchant Maiden and the Trades Maiden, both with between fifty and seventy pupils. The two similar institutions for boys were George Heriot's and George Watson's. Boys who attended these schools had their fees paid when they left to be apprenticed in a trade or to attend the University. In the 1780s there were about a hundred pupils at Heriot's and around sixty at Watson's.

The day began at the High School at eight o'clock when the janitor rang the school bell and the boys came in from the school yards, to the hall for assembly. They all sang a psalm before they went upstairs to the five classrooms, which had bare walls and floors of rough unvarnished wood, and only a little light coming in through the tiny windows. In winter the boys began and finished their day by candle-light, and became drowsy no doubt with the heat from the open coal fire. They sat at their long desks till three o'clock, with short breaks for meals at nine o'clock and midday, the only time they had for exercise. There was no time for anything else at school but book work, and the only time off was Saturday afternoon and Sunday, with a week or two of holidays in the late summer and at the end of the year during the so-called 'Daft Days'. The boys had to learn many things off by heart as the books and writing-paper, which the boys themselves had to provide, were very expensive. Text-books were bound in brown leather and had no illustrations or diagrams. Sometimes the Bible served as a reading book.

Few boys and girls can have enjoyed their schooldays. Many of their teachers were bullies who beat their pupils severely across the legs and body with the 'tawse', a stout leather belt with a frayed end.

Teachers were not trained for their work. Anybody could call himself a teacher and open a private school. Many teachers were what were called 'stickit ministers', that is students who had failed to become ministers. Salaries were so low that many masters had part-time jobs. Some were *beadles* or *session clerks* or, in the country, land surveyors. At the High School they were paid partly out of pupils' fees. Those who were popular and had large classes received more than others. Attempts to raise teachers' salaries caused a great fuss among people who objected to 'palaces for dominies'. In 1802 an Act of Parliament said that they were to receive salaries of between £16 13s 4d and £22 4s 6d.

In 1824 a new school for boys was opened in Edinburgh. The standard of education at the High School had been going down. Classes were too big and many parents were sending their sons to boarding-school in England instead. Alarmed at this state of affairs, and seeing that they could do little to improve their old school, some Edinburgh gentlemen decided that the only way to raise the standard of education in Edinburgh and keep Scots boys at home, was to start a new school.

It was called the Edinburgh Academy and was built in open country beside the Water of Leith, about ten minutes' walk from the nearest houses in the New Town. Within a few years this school became as famous as the older ones in the city. The Town Council now had to improve the High School. They moved it away from the crowded Old Town to handsome new quarters on the Calton Hill.

10　'A Hotbed of Genius'
Edinburgh's Famous Men

'Here I stand at what is called the Cross of Edinburgh, and can, in a few minutes take fifty men of genius and learning by the hand.' This is what an English visitor said in Edinburgh in the year 1769. Few other cities in the world have ever been able to deserve this claim. Another man described the city as a 'hotbed of genius'.

For about sixty years, next to London and Paris—and sometimes rather than these cities—Edinburgh was the centre of learning and new ideas in northern Europe. It produced a whole encyclopedia of knowledge: the first edition of the 'Encyclopedia Britannica' was published in Edinburgh in 1771, complete in three volumes. In 1802 appeared the 'Edinburgh Review', a magazine for which writers with new ideas wrote articles that were read by thousands. The University was crowded with students from England, whose universities—Oxford and Cambridge—had a very low standard of learning and did not admit students who were not members of the Church of England. Distinguished men of letters came to spend some time visiting the famous scholars, writers and artists of Edinburgh.

This chapter tells you about a few of these great men who lived in Edinburgh at this time and who helped to make this the 'Golden Age of Edinburgh'.

PHILOSOPHERS

A philosopher is a man who loves to think about the world and its people. Two men who lived in Edinburgh at this time were great philosophers whose ideas helped to change the lives of many people.

David Hume—by Allan Ramsay

When David Hume came back from his travels to settle down for good in his native town in 1762 he was already a famous man. After going to school and university in Edinburgh he had spent much time in London and France. He had been in turn a tutor to a mad nobleman, secretary to a general, assistant to the British ambassador in Paris and finally a very junior member of the government in London. But it was his work as a writer that had made him famous.

He was probably the first man to make money by writing history. His 'History of England' made his name. He wrote books on philosophy too. In one he put forward the startling idea that if we relied entirely on our reason in working things out we would come to the conclusion that nothing—not even ourselves—exists at all! Many people believed that reason and common sense explained completely how people thought.

David Hume made them think differently. Since then, other philosophers as well as psychologists and physicists have made use of his ideas. Some scholars say that he was the greatest of British philosophers.

Everybody liked David Hume. In France he was called 'le bon David', and he was often the chief guest at the homes of other great thinkers, such as Voltaire and Jean-Jacques Rousseau. Conversation must have been difficult, however, for he knew little French and he spoke English with a broad Scottish accent.

In Edinburgh he was the centre of a group of friends who gathered till all the hours of the night, either in the city taverns or up in his flat in fashionable James's Court in the Lawnmarket. These gentlemen were called the '*literati*' of Edinburgh. They were treated sometimes to the philosopher's own cooking at dinner, for this was one of his hobbies. You can see what he looked like on page 59.

David Hume was known as a *sceptic*, which means that he was not sure that there was a God. For most people in the eighteenth century this was unthinkable and many referred to him in horror as 'that *atheist* Hume'. This did not prevent him from being the close friend of leading ministers of the Church. The story is told about the philosopher in his fine house in the New Town where some of the streets were still without a name. One day his maidservant rushed in to tell him that someone had chalked up on the wall of his house on the corner of St Andrew Square, the words SAINT DAVID STREET—his name turned into a saint!

'Never mind, lassie,' he said, 'many a better man has been made a saint o' before.'

This is still the name of the street where he spent his last six years and died in 1776. In recent years the first of the new university buildings in George Square was named after him, the David Hume Tower.

One of the people who sadly missed the company of David Hume was his friend and fellow-philosopher, Adam Smith, who was born in Kirkcaldy in 1723. He lived there with his widowed mother until his studies took him away to the High School of Edinburgh. Then he went on to the university, first at Glasgow and then at Balliol College, Oxford. After a brief return to Edinburgh as a lecturer in English literature he

Adam Smith

went back to Glasgow as a professor at the age of twenty-eight. There he made many friends among the merchants of this thriving city. Later he travelled on the Continent as the tutor of a young nobleman on the Grand Tour. This gave him the chance to meet some great thinkers of the day in France. As a result of mixing with all these business people he wrote a book that made him world-famous. 'An Enquiry into the Nature and Causes of the Wealth of Nations' it was called, or 'The Wealth of Nations' for short.

Two years after the book was published, in 1778, Adam Smith came to live in Edinburgh, which he made his home for the rest of his life. Thanks to the generosity of a former pupil, these twelve years were very comfortably spent. He received from him a pension of £300 a year and, through his influence, he was made Commissioner of Taxes with a salary of £600.

This enabled him to live at ease in Panmure House in the Canongate, a bachelor surrounded by his 3,000 books, looked after by his old mother and cousin. They always had to hide the sugar, because he loved it so! Every morning he walked to work in the Royal Exchange, a familiar figure with his bunch of flowers from his garden and his walking cane sloped over his shoulder like a musket. An old woman is supposed to have remarked as he passed by deep in thought talking to himself, 'Hech, and he's sae weel pit on, tae!'

Many other stories are told about Adam Smith's absent-mindedness, which some people put down to the fact that he was kidnapped by gypsies at the age of three. One Sunday while he was still writing 'The Wealth of Nations' he went for a stroll in his garden in Kirkcaldy, and was suddenly startled by the sound of church bells. Still in his dressing-gown he had wandered fifteen miles along the road to Dunfermline! On another occasion while talking to a friend at breakfast, he put some buttered bread into the teapot, poured water over it and declared he had never tasted worse tea in his life. His friends among the 'literati' loved these funny ways and enjoyed listening while he talked at length on almost any subject. Not only was he full of knowledge, he was kind-hearted and had much common sense.

These close friends of his who met at his house for Sunday evening supper did not know how much he would change the world with his ideas. Adam Smith's book was read by thousands all over the world. In it he said that the proper wealth of a country does not depend upon the amount of gold or silver it possesses but upon raw materials for industry like coal and iron that can be made into useful things by the labour of skilled workmen. Gold and silver only represent wealth. Merchants in different countries should aim at trading not for gold, but for useful articles, specialising in what their countries produced best, in order that all would benefit. This trade among nations should also be left in the hands of those who understood it best—manufacturers and merchants themselves —not governments who tried to regulate it by interfering with prices and by charging customs duties. Adam Smith believed in Free Trade, that is, trade without government interference. No other writer till then had paid so much attention to the importance of trade in a country's affairs, and so he is often called 'the Father of Political Economy' the study of the wealth of the world.

Britain was the first country that had Free Trade. This was partly due to the fact that the prime minister at the time, William Pitt, understood Adam Smith's ideas and put them into practice. One evening he and Adam Smith were both guests at a friend's house. As the philosopher entered the room and apologised for being late, they all rose and the prime minister said, 'We will stand till you are seated first, for we are all your scholars.' Later prime ministers followed William Pitt's example in abolishing unnecessary restrictions on trade between Britain and other countries. In this way this country became the most prosperous in the world in the nineteenth century.

The author of 'The Wealth of Nations' lies buried in Canongate Churchyard.

ARTISTS AND ARCHITECTS

Everybody in those days liked to have his portrait painted and so there were many portrait painters living in the city. Allan Ramsay was one. He was born in Edinburgh and spent his early years there but much of his work was done in London, where he became portrait painter to King George III. The artist who spent most of his life in Edinburgh around this time was Henry Raeburn. He was born in 1756 and brought up in the little village of Stockbridge on the Water of Leith to the north of Edinburgh. Though he was left an orphan he was

Sir Henry Raeburn—by himself

cared for by his elder brother who sent him to be educated at George Heriot's School. Then he was apprenticed to a gold-smith. In his spare time he took up painting. Fortunately an artist saw some of his work and helped him with drawing lessons. Like other artists of his day he went to Italy to study. By marrying a rich widow he was able to take up painting as a full-time profession.

He became famous for the portraits he painted. All the important people in Edinburgh flocked to his studio in the New Town in York Place. He always saw about four sitters a day and then walked home to his house at Stockbridge. King George IV knighted him in 1822, the year before he died. Quite near where he lived with his dear wife, Ann, there is a delightful double row of houses—the first in Edinburgh with gardens in front of each house—that he designed himself. It is called Ann Street in her honour and it is one of the most charming in all Edinburgh.

Other Edinburgh buildings of this time were designed by one of the most famous architects in the world, Robert Adam. Like Adam Smith he went to school in Kirkcaldy and Edinburgh. In architecture we still speak about the 'Adam style' of houses. Robert Adam's father was the King's Master Builder in Scotland and his three brothers were also builders. Robert Adam travelled in France and Italy studying architecture. He brought back notebooks full of sketches of ruins of ancient buildings. Most spectacular of these drawings were the ones he made of the Palace of the Roman Emperor, Diocletian, at Split in Jugoslavia. He used these sketches when he designed houses for gentlemen who liked to live in places that looked like Greek and Roman temples. They admired the gracefulness and lightness of his designs. One gentleman, however,

Inside an Adam Country-house—the Library at Mellerstain

wanted his country house to look like an old Scottish castle and he was able to oblige him. It is called Culzean Castle and it is in Ayrshire. In Edinburgh Register House, the Old Quadrangle of the University, and the north side of Charlotte Square were all built to his design.

Robert Adam also designed the interior of houses. Everything matches in the rooms, because Robert Adam designed the fireplace, furniture and carpets.

There are still many of these Adam houses to be seen up and down the country. A few are listed in 'Things to Do' at the end of this book.

'HEAVEN-TAUGHT PLOUGHMAN'

Few people, in December 1786, noticed the arrival in Edinburgh of the man who was to become the most famous Scotsman in the world. A tall, slightly stooping figure in country clothes, he made his way to a friend's lodging in Baxter's Close in the Lawnmarket. Robert Burns, aged twenty-seven, had ridden into town to seek his fortune as a poet.

You can read about his early life with all its misfortunes as an Ayrshire farmer in another book in this series, called 'Scotland in the Age of Burns'. Just when he was preparing to emigrate to start life afresh in the West Indies, he received a letter that was to change the course of his life. Burns had recently published a book of his poems. It had been a huge success. The famous Edinburgh writer and critic, Henry Mackenzie, had praised it in a widely read journal, and the letter he received was from a blind poet, Dr Blacklock, who invited Burns to visit Edinburgh. Thus encouraged, he had come to meet men who might help him publish more of his verse.

His room in Baxter's Close was small and bare and cost three shillings a week in rent. Soon, however, he was boasting of the many parties that lords and ladies were holding in his honour. They had all read his poems and were eager to meet this farm-poet, this 'Heaven-taught ploughman' as Henry Mackenzie called him. Ladies admired his dark good looks and the gentlemen liked his good sense, though sometimes they wished that he was not quite so bold in the way he disagreed with their opinions. A publisher called William Creech agreed to publish more of his verse and many influential people promised to buy copies. One person ordered forty and another forty-two.

Robert Burns

Burns's visit to Edinburgh made him a celebrity. He was not very happy, however, in the company of the rich and the famous. He much preferred being with his friends in Dowie's Tavern off the Lawnmarket, drinking and singing with men like Willi Nicol, a master at the High School. 'Literati' like Henry Mackenzie said that he should write in English so that more people could enjoy his poetry instead of in Scots which everyone spoke but which was no longer used in writing. Burns did write poems in English, but some of them read very badly today. They sound stiff and artificial. This is because he was more at ease when he wrote in Scots, the language he spoke. Two other poets earlier in the eighteenth century had written poems in Scots. Both lived in Edinburgh: Allan Ramsay who collected poems and songs and wrote some himself, including a verse play called 'The Gentle Shepherd'; Robert Fergusson, who ended his wild life in the

Edinburgh madhouse at the age of twenty-four, after writing many verses about the city and its people, such as 'Auld Reekie' and 'Leith Races'. Burns greatly admired the works of these men; he put up a headstone over the grave of Robert Fergusson in the Canongate graveyard. By this time many of the Edinburgh 'literati' had either forgotten about the works of Ramsay and Fergusson or despised them because they were not written in English.

Burns returned for a second visit to Edinburgh within the same year. William Creech had not paid him for the new edition of poems. This time the poet lived in a flat in St. James's Square in the New Town. It was now that he met Mrs Nancy McLehose, who with her two young sons had been deserted by her worthless husband. She was a great admirer of Burns. After one meeting, which she arranged at a friend's house, she fell in love with him. Then began a curious love affair, conducted by letter for six weeks during which they could not meet, because Burns had had an accident. In their love letters she signed herself 'Clarinda' and he 'Sylvander'. But after this Burns went back to farming in Ayrshire and their correspondence petered out. The sad but beautiful love poem 'Ae fond kiss' is a reminder of their meeting.

Robert Burns's birthday is celebrated each year by Scotsmen all over the world. Lines from his poems have become everyday sayings: such as 'a man's a man for a' that', 'the best-laid schemes o' mice and men' and 'to see ourselves as others see us'. There are monuments and statues to him in Scotland and even in far-off Dunedin in New Zealand. People in all countries enjoy his songs and poems; many have been translated into other languages, for Burns wrote about things that all people can understand. And everywhere when people come to the end of a party or sing-song they join hands in friendship and sing the words that he wrote, 'Auld Lang Syne'. Burns is Scotland's national poet.

All the ladies and gentlemen of Edinburgh in the summer of 1814 were discussing one topic that for the moment seemed more important than the war in Europe. Who was 'the Great Unknown' who had written the book that everybody was reading? It was called 'Waverley' and the author remained anonymous. There had never been a book like it. The story was set in Scotland at the time of the Jacobite Rising of 1745. It was full of thrilling adventures and crowded with all kinds of interesting characters. Whoever the author was he must have had a great knowledge of history and a deep understanding of people. But who was he? While others guessed one man knew and he told no one. This was the author himself. He was a distinguished lawyer, and thought it undignified to be known as a novelist; he also loved to keep people guessing. But by the time that he admitted in public thirteen years later that he was the author of 'Waverley', it was an open secret that the most popular author in Scotland was Sir Walter Scott.

Walter Scott had been born in an old house in College Wynd in 1771. Shortly afterwards the family moved to a new house in George Square because the air in the suburbs was much healthier than in town. When he was only eighteen months old, however, he fell ill with infantile paralysis, which left him with a limp in his right leg all his life. His parents did all they could. They consulted doctors, they sent him to the health resort of Bath, and finally, to see if the country air might help him, he was sent to his grandfather's farm of Sandyknowe near Kelso in the Borders. Walking and riding over the hills helped him to grow up healthy and strong, tall and broad-shouldered. He got to know and love the Border countryside and its people, with their stories of lawless days in the past when his ancestors fought their neighbours in ancient feuds. All his days he loved this part of Scotland and never lost his strong Border accent.

When he returned to Edinburgh to go to the High School, he was already a great reader and forever astonishing his parents with his remarkable memory. After a slow start, teachers marvelled at how, for one so young, he could translate Latin poetry into English; the boys respected him as their leader in the battles, or 'bickers' as they were called, in the High School yards. And even as a boy he was well known for his gift for telling stories.

At the age of twelve he went to the University. His father wanted him to follow him in the family practice as a lawyer. Though not very keen he did as his father wanted, and began his apprenticeship after finishing university. Much of the office work was very dull, but at last, when he was twenty-one, he came out as an advocate, which meant that he could plead cases in the High Court. So successful was he that he was made the *Sheriff-substitute* of Selkirkshire.

To do his work Walter Scott had to travel a great deal about the country and so he came to know many different kinds of people. It was now that he wrote down ballads that people recited and sang for him. These ancient stories in verse had no known authors and had been passed down through generations without being written. In 1802 he published a book of them called 'The Minstrelsy of the Scottish Border'. During the next twelve years he wrote poems of his own, long ones, that made him the most popular poet in Britain. The first was called 'The Lay of the Last Minstrel', then followed 'Marmion' and 'The Lady of the Lake'. This last one was about the Highlands and described the beautiful scenery. Soon coach-loads of visitors from the Lowlands and England were tumbling along the tracks and rough roads northward to admire the countryside for themselves. Walter Scott had started tourism in the Highlands!

'Waverley' was the first of a whole series of novels. The best ones are thought to be the early ones, which are all about

Scotland: 'Guy Mannering', 'The Heart of Midlothian', 'Rob Roy' and 'Old Mortality'. All of them show how well Scott had used his years of reading history, listening to the Border tales and getting to know people. He wrote stories about English history too, in 'Ivanhoe' and 'Kenilworth', and when he brought out 'Quentin Durward', which is set in France of the fifteenth century, he became a favourite on the Continent also. As soon as the novels came out people were seen reading them in the streets. At dinner-parties in Edinburgh, the publishers used to read out ontracts from the next one to guests who could not wait for the day of publication. No wonder he was called 'the Wizard of the North'.

He was now the friend of the famous. The king made him a

Sir Walter Scott

baronet, which is how he came to be called 'Sir Walter', and when the king came to Edinburgh it was Sir Walter who made all the arrangements for welcoming him. In his Edinburgh house in Castle Street or at Abbotsford in the Borders he was always entertaining visitors himself. His country house was built near Melrose according to his instructions. It was like a castle from one of his novels, with its towers and turrets. A favourite guest was his little grandson whom he loved to tell stories from Scottish history. These he later made into a book that is called 'Tales of a Grandfather'.

In the year 1825 Scott fell deeply into debt. He had spent

The Scott Monument

money lavishly, on Abbotsford for instance, and he had lent money to his friends the publishers, John and James Ballantyne, who could not pay him back. Everyone in Edinburgh was horrified to see their most respected citizen having to sell his house and possessions in Castle Street to pay off his debts. His friends offered to help but he insisted on getting out of difficulty by his own efforts through writing. As might have been expected he made himself ill with over-work and the novels were written so quickly that they were not so good as his earlier ones. Between 1825 and 1832 he wrote five books as well as collections of short stories and other works besides. After a holiday abroad, he died at Abbotsford and was buried not far away in the family vault within the ruins of Dryburgh Abbey.

People still read the novels and poems of Sir Walter Scott. And all who enjoy historical novels by any author have him to thank, for it was he who first made them popular. Every year tourists visit Scotland and the places he made famous: the Trossachs and the Border country. In Edinburgh itself, when passengers come off the train at Waverley Station, they cannot miss one of the landmarks of the city—the monument to its most famous citizen, Sir Walter Scott.

There were many other clever people in Scotland at this time but I only have space to give you a list of a few of their discoveries, inventions and achievements: roads with lasting surfaces (John Loudon Macadam), new bridges, docks and canals (Thomas Telford), a practical steam engine (James Watt), the first iron steamship (Sir William Fairbairn), the first reaping machine (James Smith of Deanston), the steam-hammer (James Nasmyth), hydrogen-filled balloons (Joseph Black), fresh water distilled from the sea (Dr James Lind), artificial ice (Sir John Leslie), the pedal bicycle (Kirkpatrick Macmillan), a fountain pen and the rubber tyre (Robert William Thomson) and Dr James Gregory's famous 'Mixture' . . . quite a useful variety of things from a small country like Scotland within one century! Find out more about these people for yourself.

11   Pirates in the Forth

For two days watchers on the shore had followed eagerly the movements of three strange ships as they sailed into the Firth of Forth in September of 1779. Were they French? What had they come for? There was a war with the French and so they were surely up to no good. Each day reports of the strangers reached Edinburgh. They were French. Soon they could be seen from Edinburgh over to the north towards the Fife coast. By this time word was spreading fast. It was the notorious American pirate—John Paul Jones!

This was the time of the American War of Independence. Fighting between the colonists and the army of King George had been going on for three years. But to most people in Edinburgh the war was something far away which did not affect their everyday lives. Some read about the war in the newspapers weeks after the events reported had taken place, and some men attended meetings in support of the colonists in their struggle for freedom. Tobacco was up in price two shillings the pound and some farmers in the south of Scotland tried to grow their own, while many of the famous 'Tobacco Lords'—the rich Glasgow merchants, were facing ruin. Then came the news that reminded Edinburgh people that the war was nearer than they thought.

Only a man like John Paul Jones would have thought up a plan as daring as his. While their allies, the French, invaded the south of England the Americans planned to divert attention by threatening to attack Edinburgh and forcing the British government to send an army northwards. This would leave London open to attack, the French would take it, King George would ask for peace, the United States would be free and the war would be over. But was this possible with three ships and a handful of men? John Paul Jones thought it worth

74

a try.

John Paul Jones was no stranger to Scotland. He had been born about a hundred miles from Edinburgh, near Kirkbean on the shores of the Solway Firth, thirty-two years before. Until he was twenty-six he was known as John Paul. He added the name 'Jones' in the course of a highly adventurous career as a sailor and a trader on ships plying between Britain and the West Indies. At twenty-one, after eight years afloat, he was ship's master. Five years later he was part-owner of a ship, a successful trader and a skilled navigator. During a mutiny in the West Indies he killed a man. Fearing that he would not get a fair trial, he fled to Virginia. This was when he took the name Jones. Soon after this, fighting broke out in 1776 between the American colonists and the forces of the King. Paul Jones joined the tiny American navy, taking part in the first naval battle in the war, and later commanding his own ship. He is called the Founder of the United States Navy. When the French joined the war on the side of the Americans against their old enemies the British, Paul Jones was sent to France to take charge of a French ship.

In the spring of 1778 Paul Jones began raiding the west coast of Britain. One day he attacked the port of Whitehaven, in Cumberland, the next he landed a party near his birthplace to capture the Earl of Selkirk, a local laird. The nobleman escaped being held to ransom but his wife was at home, and was very politely required to hand over the household silver. Both times the raiders escaped unscathed. This episode earned for Paul Jones a reputation in America and France for skill and daring, and in Britain as a rebel and a pirate, ruthless and cruel.

This was the man who was now in the Firth of Forth with three ships—the 'Bonhomme Richard', the 'Pallas' and the 'Vengeance'. He sailed in the 'Bonhomme Richard', a 40-gun frigate of 850 to 900 tons. His crews were mainly Americans and Englishmen, but included men of many nationalities. There were also 137 French marines on board for the plan that was only now revealed to his captains. They would land at Leith and present a demand for £200,000. If the townsfolk did not pay up the port would be burnt to ashes. There was nothing to stop him carrying out this threat, it seemed. There was no sizeable warship in the Forth and the guns of Edinburgh Castle could not fire far enough out to sea. The city was at the mercy of John Paul Jones.

Not knowing these plans but fearing the worst, the people of Edinburgh and the country round the Forth were in a terrible turmoil. Some fled inland with all their possessions but most waited for the invader to come. Many thought that the raiders would not dare to land. Not taking any chances, seamen in Leith formed companies of ten to mount a twenty-four hour watch on the harbour and called for muskets from Edinburgh. Along the shore batteries of thirty guns were set up. Hurriedly a message was sent to Perth for more. Meanwhile over in Fife Sir John Anstruther sent out some men in his yacht to borrow some gunpowder for his brass cannon from HMS 'Romney' off-shore. While the crew returned with the powder, the master was invited below to meet the captain who had obliged him so readily. There he found himself face to face with Paul Jones on board his own ship! The ship's log tells the story briefly like this: 'There come a Shore Boat with 5 Men in hit. At $\frac{1}{2}$ past 5 p.m. sent 4 of them a Shore again and sent 1 Cask of Powder withem.'

The next day, Sunday, in Kirkcaldy, the Reverend Mr Shirra prepared as usual for morning service. The congregation, however, too busy to attend church, watched in horrified silence the American ships at anchor a mile off shore. The good minister called for a chair and proceeded with the service on the beach. He prayed on God to send a wind to blow away the 'vile pirate' and threatened to sit until the tide came in if his prayer was not answered. Suddenly—and fortunately for Mr Shirra—to the amazement of the congregation, his prayer seemed to be answered. Before their eyes the enemy ships were weighing anchor and moving off. Within firing range of Leith and as the landing-party prepared to go ashore, the intruders had found themselves caught in 'a sudden and violent storm' as Paul Jones called it. In confusion the whole scheme was abandoned as the American ships were blown down the Forth into the open sea.

No one could believe his eyes, but everybody thanked God and heaved a sigh of relief, that is except the people in the towns along the north-east coast of England. The Americans fell in with a British fleet of forty ships coming home from the Baltic with valuable ship's stores. Off Flamborough Head Paul Jones engaged some of them in battle. The 'Bonhomme Richard' was sunk and H.M.S. 'Serapis' having surrendered, Paul Jones made off in her to friendly Holland.

John Paul Jones had passed out of Edinburgh's history. He went on to be honoured in America and also by the French. Everywhere ladies loved his charm and good looks. A famous sculptor made a bust of him, which shows us what he looked like. He had many more adventures in America and Europe. When he commanded a Russian fleet against the Turks he was a rear-admiral and known as Pavel Ivanovitch. Most of the time, however, he lived in France, though in 1791 he visited England—as a friend

Courtesy, Museum of Fine Arts, Boston
John Paul Jones

77

now tnat the war was long over. The next year he died in Paris.

The scare had taught the citizens of Edinburgh a lesson. They would have to be better prepared for attack from the sea in any future war. So the Town Council built a fort at Leith for a hundred soldiers and eight 24-pounder guns. A regiment was raised known as the Defensive Band of Volunteers. Edinburgh was ready for any invader.

12   Friend of the People

Few people in 1793 would have said that the slightly built young man with fair hair and blue eyes looked like a dangerous criminal as he stood in the High Court in Parliament Hall. Yet Thomas Muir of Huntershill, near Glasgow, was on trial for his life, charged with sedition, accused of plotting to overthrow the government.

These were grave times. In France, Revolutionaries had brought down the government and in its place had set up a new one to provide 'Liberty, Equality and Fraternity'. Sweeping changes were taking place, in which those who resisted the Revolutionaries were put to death. People in Britain followed these events with great interest. Some regarded the changes with horror, while others approved of them. Thomas Muir was one of these because he thought that similar changes were needed in this country. A man like Thomas Muir who wanted great changes made was known as a Radical. Many Radicals were members of associations and clubs to help to urge on the changes they wanted. Thomas Muir was a leader of the one called 'the society of the Friends of the People'. Its members came from all walks of life: lairds and lawyers, labourers and craftsmen. Each paid a subscription of a shilling a year, and they met to discuss matters of urgent interest and press the

Thomas Muir

government to agree to improving the way the country was run. They wanted to reform Parliament, to make it represent the people of the country better than it did at that time. At that time only men who owned a certain amount of property had the right to vote for members of parliament, and so Parliament passed laws that benefited them, while most people had no say in the country's affairs. Thomas Muir and his friends wanted all men—and not only property owners—to be given the right to vote.

There was need to reform the way that burghs were run too. The councils were not elected by the townsfolk but were made up of men belonging to prominent local families who had been appointed by other members of the town councils. Such men often used their positions as town councillors for their own selfish ends, such as using the burgh's money or buying up land from the burgh at give-away prices. No proper accounts were kept to check this and so the people did not know what was being done with their money. Altogether, the burghs were very corrupt and many, including Edinburgh, were falling into debt.

The rebellion of the American colonists had shown people in this country that changes could be made in the government of their country. Then came the French Revolution. Radicals in Britain took heart. Perhaps there would be more support for their cause. Then the revolutionaries in France turned to violence to get their way, seizing private property and putting innocent people to death. Britain went to war with the French to prevent them from spreading revolution. Most people in Britain disliked the bloodshed of the Revolution, and so societies like the Friends of the People began to lose support. There were scenes of violence in Edinburgh as well as in other parts of the country. Jeering mobs attacked soldiers in the High Street on the King's Birthday. The windows of leading citizens were smashed, and down in Leith sailors went on

One of the City Guard with his Lochaber Axe

strike for more pay. Honest citizens were alarmed because there was no proper police-force; the City Guard was a laughing-stock; many of their members were too old and frail to carry their long Lochaber axes from the Guard House in the High Street. Was there going to be a revolution in Scotland?

One man at least was determined that there would be nothing of the sort. This was Henry Dundas, M.P. for Edinburgh and member of the government of William Pitt. As Home Secretary it was his responsibility to see that law and order were respected. To find out possible trouble-makers he used spies and opened the letters of people he suspected. Finally he decided that a dangerous ringleader of revolutionaries was Thomas Muir, who was therefore arrested and charged with sedition while on his way to Edinburgh on 2 January 1793.

Between the time of his arrest and the opening of his trial many things happened that affected the verdict. Having been released on bail he went to France and was not back in time for his trial in Edinburgh. Meanwhile the French had executed their king and war between Britain and France had been declared. So when Muir finally made his way back to Scotland hardly anybody believed his story that he had gone to France to persuade the French not to put their king to death and that he had been held up by the outbreak of war.

The trial of Thomas Muir is one of the most famous in Scottish history. The court-room that August was filled with people who were eager to see this 'demon of mischief' as Dundas called him. From the start he had hardly a chance of a fair hearing. The Lord Advocate, who acted as prosecutor on behalf of the Crown, was a nephew of Henry Dundas, and based his case on the flimsiest of evidence. The jury of fifteen men were known to be enemies of the prisoner, and the judge, who ought to have been fair was openly hostile. This was the famous Lord Braxfield, who was noted for his dislike of all revolutionary ideas and his coarse sense of humour. 'They would a' be the muckle better o' being hangit', he was heard to say in his broad Scottish tongue about reformers. During this trial he whispered one day to one of the members of the jury, 'Come awa' Maister Horner, come awa' and help us to hang ane o' thae damned scoondrels'.

With such a judge and jury, though he defended himself with great skill, it is little wonder that Thomas Muir was found guilty. But no one was expecting the sentence the judge gave him—fourteen years as a convict in New South Wales at Botany Bay. Even the jurymen thought this harsh. It shows how scared people like Lord Braxfield were of revolution. The friends of Thomas Muir tried to persuade Parliament to intervene but without success. In America and in France he was praised as a hero and a martyr in the cause of freedom. Inspired by his example, Robert Burns wrote 'Scots wha hae', which he imagined to be what King Robert the Bruce said to his soldiers before the Battle of Bannockburn. Charles James Fox, a famous politician of the time and leading opponent of the government, summed up the feelings of many when he remarked, 'God help the people who have such judges.'

To avoid the angry Edinburgh mob who were on his side, Thomas Muir was quickly shipped to London in chains and there transferred to a convict hulk for the journey to Australia.

A Convict Hulk

On board were prisoners of all sorts, forgers and thieves as well as three others who had been convicted for political offences—Thomas Fyshe Palmer, William Skirving and Maurice Margarot. They arrived in Australia in October 1794, a year later.

This was not the end of the story of Thomas Muir, it was only the beginning of a series of adventures that read like a story in fiction. In New South Wales he was able to buy a small farm where he worked contentedly. One day, however, in February 1796 an American ship, the 'Otter' put in for food and water. Unknown to him friends in New York had specially commissioned the ship for his escape. He slipped on board and sailed away to freedom. Off the coast of North America a British warship was sighted, so he transferred to a Spanish ship that landed him in Mexico, then a Spanish colony. Crossing the country with help from the viceroy, he found himself in Havana in Cuba. For four months he was kept in prison until he was put on board a vessel returning to Spain. Surely now, he thought, he would be safe, for Spain was an ally of France and at war with Britain.

Meanwhile, word of Thomas Muir's whereabouts had reached the British. At the entrance to Cadiz harbour two of their warships attacked the one on which he was known to be. In the hand-to-hand fighting Muir was very badly injured, and when the Spanish ship was captured he was taken for dead. But for a ship's doctor who recognised him from his schooldays he would have been thrown overboard. Instead he was sent ashore for treatment. From here he was taken to France on the instructions of the French government. He was free and safe at last.

For the rest of his days he lived in France. He was welcomed like a hero. 'Long live the defender of Liberty!' shouted the crowds, and everywhere pictures of him were on display. There were speeches and celebrations in his honour. He worked for the French government writing pamphlets and articles against his own country and other enemies of the Revolution. If the French had ever succeeded in stirring up revolution in Britain they would probably have made Thomas Muir a member of the revolutionary government of Scotland.

But there was no revolution in Britain. Henry Dundas was an efficient man and most people were too loyal to their country. Thomas Muir died in France in January 1799, worn out with ill-health and fatigue in the cause of freedom for the people.

The wars against the French went on till 1815. There are many reminders in the city still of these grim times of revolution and war. When the war was over it was decided to put up a national monument to commemorate those who died in the fighting. It stands on the Calton Hill, a copy of the Parthenon, the famous temple in Athens; but it is unfinished because there was never enough money to complete it and so it is called 'Edinburgh's Disgrace'. Near the National Monument

'Edinburgh's Disgrace'

stands the Nelson Tower; and there are also Trafalgar Street and Nelson Street. The Duke of Wellington is commemorated by a mounted statue near Waterloo Place. There are Howe Street, Abercrombie Place and Pitt Street. A statue of Pitt stands in George Street. You can find also a street named after Henry Dundas and a statue of him on top of a column over a hundred feet high in St Andrew Square. This is called the Melville Column because Dundas was made Viscount Mel-

The Melville Column

ville. A little to the east in the Calton graveyard stands a less conspicuous souvenir of this period: a tall *obelisk* with the following words inscribed at the base:

86

TO

THE MEMORY OF

THOMAS MUIR

THOMAS FYSHE PALMER

WILLIAM SKIRVING

MAURICE MARGAROT

AND

JOSEPH GERRALD

Erected by the Friends of Parliamentary Reform
in England and Scotland
1844

I have devoted myself to the cause of the People. It
is a good cause—it shall ultimately prevail—it shall
finally triumph. 30 VIII 93.

There is a ring of triumph in these words spoken by Thomas
Muir at his trial. By the time the monument was raised
Parliament had been reformed and so had town councils.
Thomas Muir, the 'Friend of the People' had not suffered in
vain.

The Calton Hill, showing the Martyrs' Obelisk, the Nelson Monument and other buildings

13   'Carle, now the King's Come'

Deep in the Highlands in an old country house called the
Doune, two young ladies prepared to go on a long journey.
The Misses Jane and Mary Grant, aged twenty-one and
eighteen, daughters of John Peter Grant of Rothiemurchus,
Inverness-shire, were preparing to go with their brother,
William, on the hundred-mile journey to Edinburgh.

The Grant family were about to make a most extraordinary
visit. They were going to see the King. His Majesty, King
George the Fourth had announced in a letter to the Lord
Provost of Edinburgh in July that he was going to visit the
city in the following month. Nowadays people are quite
accustomed to seeing members of the Royal Family, either in
person or in pictures, but for about 110 years no reigning
monarch ever came to Scotland. So now in 1822 the news of
the visit of King George IV to Edinburgh caused a sensation.
Everybody in Scotland wanted to see him and so in thousands
they flocked to Edinburgh.

It was on 8 August that the Misses Grant set off for Edinburgh to see the king. The coach sped through the Highlands
to Perth and on through Kinross and over the Forth in the
new steam ferry-boat, arriving in Edinburgh on Saturday, two
days later. Possibly they chatted about the King. He had been
on the throne for two years and was now fifty-eight. Though
as a young man ladies had found him very handsome, he was
now so stout that he had to wear stays. People told the most
scandalous stories about his private life and many of them were
true. For many years the King had lived apart from his wife,
Queen Caroline, and had tried to divorce her. At his coro-
nation in Westminster Abbey he had even forbidden her to
attend and she was sent away when she tried to get in. He
had spent a fortune, collecting works of art and building a

fantastic house for himself—the Pavilion at Brighton—as well as eating, drinking and gambling. This was going on at a time of great hardship in the country, when many could hardly afford a loaf of bread or a roof over their heads. Work was scarce and wages were low. There was unrest and discontent all over the country, especially in the industrial Midlands of England and the west of Scotland.

Possibly it was to make the King popular again that Sir Walter Scott suggested the royal visit. For all his faults, King George was a charming person with very winning ways. He liked the idea of coming to Scotland. The citizens of Edinburgh had a month to prepare.

When the Grants arrived at their uncle's house in the New Town they found the whole of Edinburgh in a state of great excitement. Nobody could speak of anything else, it seemed, as they prepared for the King's visit. Whenever they ran into difficulties they turned to Sir Walter Scott, who was in charge of the arrangements.

While they waited for the King to come, the Grant ladies had plenty to do. As they were among the thousands who had been invited to meet His Majesty, they had to see to their Court dresses and to practice their curtsies. There was always something to watch. Workmen were busy everywhere night and day, piping water and gas into Holyrood Palace, laying new roads and clearing away old houses. The cannon at the Castle were given a new coat of paint and repairs in the stonework were carried out there and in St. Giles's Cathedral. In the main streets new gas lamps were installed. For the bonfires and fireworks display horses hauled up cartloads of wood to the top of Arthur's Seat. Out on the Bass Rock men struggled to erect six cannon and a flag-pole forty feet high for a royal salute when the King's ships entered the Firth of Forth. There was great stir also at Dalkeith, six miles from Edinburgh, at the home of the Duke of Buccleuch where His

Majesty was to reside. A special dairy and laundry were set up and a road was redirected. Soldiers had to be stationed in the little town, which made it more difficult to provide rooms for the visitors in inns and private houses. Leith, where the King would arrive, prepared too.

As the day of the King's arrival drew near visitors from all over the country poured into Edinburgh. A newspaper in Glasgow reported:

'Glasgow, as far as we can learn, will be almost deserted on the occasion—every vehicle of conveyance is fully employed and engaged for coming days. Extra boats on the canal are insufficient for the number of passengers. Where the moving mass from all corners of the land are to stow themselves when in Edinburgh we know not. Many, we understand, are provided with or are providing themselves with tents, and intend to *bivouac* in the fields.'

The writer in the newspaper was right. The Calton Hill and the Salisbury Crags were littered with the tents of the visitors unable to afford the charges demanded by the hotel-keepers who soon filled their rooms with guests who could. Food prices rose.

Opposite Princes Street on the slopes of the Castle Hill there were other campers: Highland clansmen, the followers, the 'tails' of leading Highland chieftains. They created a sensation in their kilts, which not so long ago they had been forbidden by law to wear, as they marched into town to the bagpipes playing 'The Campbells are coming'. The days dragged, the crowds grew impatient as they gathered round the mailcoach from London for news of the King. Eagerly they scanned the horizon for sign of his ships. Suppose he had changed his mind and was not coming at all!

Then suddenly, on the afternoon of Wednesday 14 August 1822, bursts of cannon fire resounded through the town. The King! It was the King! He had come at last! Yonder were his ships coming to anchor off Leith—the King's yacht the 'Royal George', accompanied by two steamships which had towed her part of the way, with an escort of ships from the Royal Navy. The rain poured down. The crowds, in their best clothes, had waited too long, however, to be daunted by the weather, so they rushed to the stands set up along the route the king would take. Even when His Majesty decided to postpone his entry until the next day many loyal citizens still remained out in the rain watching for any movement from the royal yacht, while some even rowed out hoping to catch a glimpse of him.

Next morning the rain had stopped. The city looked beautiful. Everyone was up early. Gentlemen were wearing the special uniform of blue coat, white vest and white pantaloons. This is how the Misses Grant described the day in a letter home to their mother, brother and sister Elizabeth who was not well enough to travel,

> 'We were off at ten equipped as yesterday. The servants in full dress liveries, the horses decorated with new scarlet *cockades* and cloth paddings under the saddles of their bright rubbed harness. It was a lovely morning, sun shining splendidly; the heavens bright and clear; the whole scene gay and smiling . . . All the stages and platforms crowded with people; the windows of each tall house full to the very top; the Calton Hill covered with tents and spectators; the streets crowded on each side, and a broad empty space lined with *yeomanry* left in the middle for the coming procession. Even the roofs of the houses were covered with people standing upright by the chimneys or clinging where they could; the doors and steps of the houses all full; boys seated on the tops of the lamp posts and hanging up the posts.'

The ladies had a wonderful view of the route from Leith and were very near the spot where the King was officially welcomed to Edinburgh. They go on to say:

'We were seated for two hours before the procession began to appear, but I was well amused with watching the crowds passing up and down, the carriages driving up and about, horsemen hurrying here and there and so on. We saw quantities of people we knew hurrying to their several stands or seats.'

Leith Harbour

Just after midday the King had stepped ashore in the uniform of Admiral of the Fleet from the royal barge to a terrific noise of welcome. Cannon banged out, bagpipes droned and a band from the Canongate played 'God Save the King'. There was cheering on every side from people standing at windows, on rooftops, hanging from ships' rigging and also holding on to the upturned drawbridge over the Water of Leith. Lined up on the Shore, as the quayside at Leith is called, stood a welcoming group of dignitaries, the Leith magistrates to the fore, along with soldiers and archers of the Royal Bodyguard in Scotland in their distinctive uniforms of green with feathered caps. After the ceremony of welcome to Scotland, the procession moved off through Leith, troops, trumpeters and pipers with important people in open carriages. Welcoming banners streamed from the houses and arches decked with flags and flowers. The banners read, 'O HAPPY DAY', 'HAIL SCOTIA'S KING' and 'WELCOME G IV R'.

At the top of Leith Walk(which was so broad it might have been made for occasions like this) the procession halted and the Lord Provost solemnly bade the King welcome to Edinburgh. Then the cavalcade moved on, up Picardy Place and into York Place. This is how the Misses Grant described the scene:

> 'The procession was beautiful. I think the king's carriage splendid; he was very gracious and each lady in our three houses declared he gave her a particular bow . . . I saw him take off his hat very gracefully, and everybody said he looked quite pleased and delighted; but when he got further through the town, they complained that he looked fagged and did not raise his hat quite so high.'

The carriages passed on through St Andrew Square to Princes Street, where they turned up past the Calton Hill and down towards Holyrood. Here the King stepped down to the deafening roar of cannon for another ceremony of welcome. The King had indeed come.

There are many poems and songs that were specially written for this special occasion. Here is part of one that Sir Walter Scott composed:

CARLE, NOW THE KING'S COME

> The news has flown frae mouth to mouth,
> The North for ance has bang'd the South;
> The de'il a Scotsman's die o' drouth,
>   *Carle*, now the King's come!

Chorus
Carle, now the King's come!
Carle, now the King's come!
Thou shalt dance, and I will sing,
     Carle, now the King's come!

Thirty-seven more verses like this tell how happy the Scots were to see their King.

For the next fortnight Edinburgh was like a swarm of bees buzzing round its hive. The King held receptions at the Palace, he took part in a procession from the Palace to the Castle—which for many was the highlight of the whole visit because they saw the ancient honours of Scotland, the crown, sceptre

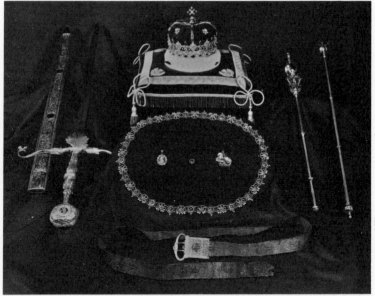

The Honours of Scotland

and sword of state, being solemnly carried—he reviewed troops on the sands at Portobello, he worshipped at St. Giles's, he went to two splendid balls in the Assembly Rooms, was present at the Theatre Royal for a special performance of a play based on Sir Walter Scott's novel, 'Rob Roy', and he attended a sumptuous banquet given in his honour by the Town Council in Parliament Hall. At night the city was ablaze with illuminations. Even the gasworks chimney in the Canongate was decorated with a glistening crown! Nobody could stay indoors: there was too much going on to sleep! The night the King arrived thousands were out in their best clothes, to watch the dancing in the streets and the fireworks displays to the sound of cannon and bursts of gunfire. We go back to the letters of the Misses Grant and read:

> 'Every street in every corner of the town was literally filled with people of every rank; not merely the footways on each side but the broad pavement [roadway] held a moving mass whichever way you went. Most of the houses were simply lighted with candles, some one in every pane; others in figures; these certainly look best on the whole, and make a better show than lamps.'

Everybody was well behaved and nobody was drunk or 'uncivil', they tell us.

All the arrangements went off according to plan, though the weather was not always kind. Crowds were soaked on the day of the procession to the Castle; so those who had paid up to a hundred guineas for a seat at a window overlooking the Royal Mile must have thought the price was worth paying to stay dry.

Then came the day of the King's departure, the 29th. He drove out to see the Earl of Hopetoun at Hopetoun House and left by sea in the late afternoon from Port Edgar. To the accompaniment of a thundering royal salute, the king's squadron left behind in the Forth a fleet of pleasure boats, whose passengers cheered and waved flags as they said farewell to their sovereign.

From all accounts the King seemed to enjoy himself immensely. He loved Edinburgh and the crowds in the streets who were so friendly, unlike the London crowds who turned out to shout rude things at him. For most people the visit had come up to expectations. Some Edinburgh people, however, said that Sir Walter had given the Highlanders too big a part to play in the festivities. There was tartan everywhere. Even the King appeared in it and so did his friend the Lord Mayor of London. Both men were very fat and they created a sensation in full Highland rig—kilt, sporran and feathered hat, with legs covered with pink tights. Cartoonists seized on this to make fun of the King. Some ladies were saying that they hoped he would not wear his kilt at the Assembly Rooms when one jokingly remarked, 'Since his stay will be so short, the more we see of him the better!'

Making fun of the King in his Kilt

The Misses Grant were not disappointed. They attended most of the royal functions. To the delight of their father they were considered to be the most attractive of all the ladies presented to the King. Perhaps this is why he sent His Majesty thirty brace of ptarmigan with a dozen bottles of his best Glenlivet when he learned that this was his favourite brand of whisky. And when it was all over they had some wonderful stories to tell that they had not included in their letters home to the family in Inverness-shire.

King George did not return to Scotland, but there are many reminders of his visit. The spot where he landed at Leith is still marked with an iron plate with the words 'GEO IV—O FELICEM DIEM' (George IV—O Happy Day). His statue stands at the top of Hanover Street and a bridge is called after him.

In another way, too, we are reminded of this royal visit. Until his time the kilt was worn only by Highlanders. George IV helped to popularise the kilt and tartan. Soon, Lowlanders with only the remotest connection with the Highlands would be wearing the kilt, and ladies in the height of fashion in Paris would be proud of their tartan dresses. Some of the designs of these tartans are quite old, but many go back no further than 1822.

14   The Body-Snatchers

'Doun the close and up the stair,
But an' ben wi' Burke and Hare.
Burke's the butcher, Hare's the thief,
Knox the man that buys the beef.'

This is an old rhyme that comes from Edinburgh. It refers to three men who took part in some gruesome adventures towards the end of the city's Golden Age. At least two plays and one short story have been written about these three characters, Dr Robert Knox and the murderers, Burke and Hare.

By the nineteenth century Edinburgh had grown famous for the training of doctors and surgeons. There were so many medical students, however, that it was hard to provide enough bodies for *dissecting* in their anatomy lectures. The regular supply was restricted by law, but it was a well-known fact that surgeons obtained bodies by other means. The men who supplied them were known as 'Resurrectionists' or 'Body-snatchers'. Under cover of darkness these desperate men would dig up coffins and take out the bodies of people who had just been buried. Taking the greatest of pains to leave no trace or make the slightest noise, they would push the corpse into a sack or box and take it to a willing customer who paid up and asked no questions. Relatives of newly dead people were so alarmed that they sometimes placed a metal grille over the graves to prevent bodies being stolen. These are called mort-safes and can still be seen in old cemeteries. Night-watchmen were employed too, and harmed with a *blunderbuss* to ward off raiders. But the horrible plunder of graves still went on.

One lecturer in anatomy never seemed to be short of fresh corpses. Dr Robert Knox did not lecture at the University but

A Mortsafe

privately to hundreds of eager students in Surgeons Square near the Old Infirmary. Though not a pleasant man to look at, his students greatly respected his skill as a surgeon. Then one day in class, some of his students were shocked when they recognised the body before them on the dissecting table. It was the body of Mary Paterson, a girl of eighteen, whom many of them knew and had seen recently in good health and spirits. How on earth had she come to be here? On another occasion there was another surprise when there turned up in Dr Knox's class-room the body of another well-known figure of the Edinburgh streets. This was Daft Jamie, a well-built simple soul of nineteen, who wandered about Edinburgh, getting board and lodging from anybody who took pity on him. He was popular so he was strong and healthy. How had he died? It was only when the police arrested and charged with murder two men who came from the West Port that the deaths of Mary Paterson and Daft Jamie were linked with the mystery of how Dr Knox came by his supply of fresh bodies.

The trial of the two men, Burke and Hare, one of the most famous in Scottish legal history, began on Christmas Eve 1829. They made an evil-looking pair: Hare, tall and thin with a leering expression on his face, and Burke, small, thick-set and dark. The most eminent lawyers of the day took part and every inch of space was taken up with interested onlookers. Only Burke, along with his wife, stood trial; Hare and his wife had turned King's evidence, which means that they had agreed to give evidence for the Crown against their friends. Without their help there would not have been enough evidence to convict the other two.

The crowd in court and the people who read it in their newspapers were horrified at the story that came out in the trial. It all started when Burke, a feckless cobbler, took lodgings in Hare's house in the West Port. One day one of Hare's lodgers, an old soldier, died, owing £4 in rent. The two men decided to get the money by selling the old man's corpse to Dr. Knox. Soon Burke and Hare were in business. They sold the bodies of about fifteen more people, luckless victims whom they lured to death by making them drunk and then suffocating them. They thrust the bodies into a tea-chest and carted them to Dr Knox who paid them for each corpse £10 in winter and £8 in summer. He does not seem to have asked them where the goods came from; he was presumably only too keen to have them.

The victims were all people whom nobody missed or cared about—except Mary Paterson and Daft Jamie. Success had made the murderers bold and careless. But it was not the murder of these well-known persons that led to the arrest of Burke and Hare, but the murder of a little old Irishwoman who had only recently come to Edinburgh with her grandson. The old woman's body was discovered under a pile of straw on a bed in Burke's house by two lodgers who were suspicious of what went on there.

When the judge announced that Burke was found guilty the crowd in court burst into cheering. They were only sorry that Hare too could not be punished for his part in the crimes; but he was protected by the law for being the chief witness for the Crown. Burke's wife got off also; the jury brought in a verdict of 'Not proven', which is possible under Scots law but not in English law.

A few days later Burke was hanged in the Lawnmarket

The Execution of Burke

before a crowd of about 20,000 who stood in the rain to watch. They had been gathering since the gallows were put up the night before. A roar of hatred went up and when the body was cut down the police had to hold the crowd back from grabbing hold of it. Some scrambled to seize bits of the rope for souvenirs. Then, according to the rest of the judge's sentence, Burke's body was taken away to be dissected in public. When this was being carried out a riot took place as students clamoured to get in.

Though the others involved in the murders escaped hanging they all had to be protected from the crowds of people who wanted to *lynch* them. Hare and Burke's wife were both chased over the Border into England and Mrs Hare was last seen on the boat to Belfast. As for Dr Knox, a mob of people burned his *effigy* and smashed the windows of his house at Newington on the south side of town. He escaped by the back door and fled from the city. An enquiry had been held that cleared his name of being connected with the murders or being responsible for them in any way, but his students deserted him and no one who knew about his past would employ him. He died in London in 1862.

The case of Burke and Hare showed clearly that there were two faces of Edinburgh in its Golden Age. Many respectable people in the New Town found out what they did not know—or shut their eyes to—about life in their own city, in the slums of the old part, with its dens of vice, where the poor Irishmen were obliged to live when they came to work on the Union Canal that ran from Edinburgh to Falkirk. Perhaps the trial of Burke and Hare led to the clearing away of many of the slums in the middle of the last century. It certainly ended the work of the Body-snatchers for the law was changed to make sure that surgeons got a proper supply of bodies for dissecting.

By this time the Golden Age of Edinburgh was drawing to a close. The Town Council was bankrupt and people were demanding that it be reformed. The death of Sir Walter Scott in 1832 robbed the city of the last of its great men. Fewer eminent men were now living there. Most of them went to London or other parts of the world. Lords and ladies were moving out of Edinburgh and leaving their dignified mansions to be turned into shops, flats, hotels, nursing-homes and offices. Edinburgh became a centre for business, a city of breweries and biscuit factories. In 1831 the railway came and later it was brought right into the heart of the city through Princes Street Gardens. Gradually the soot from the railway engines and the factory chimneys seeped into the stone which turned the buildings from light brown to dull grey and black. In more ways than one Edinburgh's Golden Age was over.

THINGS TO DO

1. Find out about modern New Towns: where they are and what they look like. Try to visit one. If you live in a New Town find out how different yours is from an old one.
2. Draw a map of your town or district and show the different parts according to the age of the buildings. Use different colours or shading for each part.
3. Write a conversation between two Edinburgh citizens discussing what they thought was good and bad about the changes taking place in their city in the eighteenth century.
4. Make a frieze, entitled 'Edinburgh in its Golden Age', showing the main streets and buildings, people at work and play and some of the famous men. Use the illustrations in the book to help you.
5. Write plays or draw strip cartoons about the adventures of Thomas Muir and the exploits of John Paul Jones.
6. Try to carry out the recipe for Whipped Syllabub on page 39. There are many more old Scottish recipes in 'The Scots Kitchen' by F. Marian McNeill.
7. Edinburgh's new streets were called after famous people and events. Find out how the streets in your town got their names.
8. At the end of term you may put on in class an 'Edinburgh Entertainment'. Here is a suggested programme:
   - *Songs:* 'Caller Herring' (Lady Nairne)
     'Within a Mile of Edinburgh Toun' (d'Urfrey)
   - *Dances:* 'The Flowers of Edinburgh'
     'The New Town of Edinburgh'
   - *Verse:* 'Braid Claith' (Fergusson)
     'Ae Fond Kiss' (Burns)
9. Here are lists of places you may like to visit:

   In Edinburgh
   The Castle, the Royal Mile and the Palace of Holyroodhouse.
   Charlotte Square in the New Town.
   Museums: Huntly House, Canongate; Museum of Antiquities, Queen Street; Lady Stair's House, Lawnmarket.
   Art Galleries: The National Gallery, Princes Street; National Portrait Gallery, Queen Street.

   Houses designed by Robert Adam and his Father
   Hopetoun House, West Lothian
   Culzean Castle, Ayrshire
   Mellerstain, Berwickshire
   Kenwood House, Hampstead.

FURTHER READING

BARCLAY, J. B., *Edinburgh*. Black.

CHAMBERS, ROBERT, *Traditions of Edinburgh*. Chambers

GRAHAM, H. G., *The Social Life of Scotland in the Eighteenth Century*. Black

GRANT, JAMES, *Old and New Edinburgh*. Cassell

KAY, JOHN, *Edinburgh Portraits*

LINDSAY, IAN G., *Georgian Edinburgh*. Oliver & Boyd

MCNEILL, F., MARIAN, *The Scots Kitchen*. Blackie

MACPHAIL, I. M. M., *A History of Scotland*. Arnold

PLANT, MARJORIE, *The Domestic Life of Scotland in the Eighteenth Century*. Edinburgh University Press.

SINCLAIR, SIR JOHN, ED., *The Statistical Account of Scotland*

WISEMAN, H. & EASSON, I., *Scots Song Books*, 4 vols. Nelson

YOUNG, DOUGLAS, *Edinburgh in the Age of Sir Walter Scott*. University of Oklahoma Press.

YOUNGSON, A. J., *The Making of Classical Edinburgh*. Edinburgh University Press

Many more books written about Scotland around this time are listed in *Scottish Books: a Brief Bibliography for Teachers and General Readers;* the Saltire Society, Gladstone's Land, Lawnmarket, Edinburgh.

GLOSSARY

accompt, old word for account or bill
advocate, Scottish barrister
atheist, one who does not believe in God
aumry, Scottish word for ambry, old word for cupboard
beadle, church officer in Scotland
betwixt, between
bivouac, to camp out
blunderbuss, old-fashioned short hand-gun
carle, man
chandelier, elaborate frame with many branches to hold candles
close, alley in a town
cockade, rosette worn on hat
collops, pieces of meat
commendation, praise
contrived, managed
coom-ceiling, one that slopes from the wall
cornice, plaster moulding round a ceiling
curling, sliding heavy smooth stones over a sheet of ice
debris, rubbish
declivities, slopes
delft, kind of earthenware
dilapidated, ruined
dissect, to cut up in pieces
diverse, different
edifice, building
effigy, dummy made to look like a person
ell, cloth measure equal to $1\frac{1}{4}$ yd.
escritoire, writing-desk
executed, carried out
extensive, wide
extremity, end
firkin, small barrel
flummery, kind of blancmange
fraternity, society or brotherhood
hackney carriage, four-wheeled one for hire
hirple, to walk with a limp
imprimis, firstly
indweller, inhabitant
intersected, cut across
'literati', learned men
Lord Justice-Clerk, second highest judge in Scotland
lord of session, Scottish High Court judge

Lord President, highest judge in Scotland
lynch, to judge and put to death without a trial
manifest, show clearly
mantua-maker, dressmaker
mews, stables
milliner, dealer in headwear and fancy goods
minuet, slow, graceful dance
mutchkin, measure equal to an English pint
nankeen, buff-coloured cotton cloth
obelisk, tall, four-sided tapering stone pillar with a pyramid at the top
office, job
pantaloons, trouserlike garments
pantile, curved roof-tile
parlour, sitting-room
pattens, soles mounted on iron rings to keep shoes from getting wet
periodical, magazine that comes out regularly
pitcher, large jug
pomatum, hair-cream made from fat
porter, dark brown beer
portico, porch with pillars
posset, hot spiced milk curdled with ale or wine
project, plan
prospect, view
quadrangle, four-sided figure
room-setter, boarding-house keeper
sceptic, one who questions beliefs
sedan chair, a chair carried on poles by two chairmen
session clerk, secretary to Scottish kirk session
sheriff-substitute, local judge in Scotland
spinet, early form of piano
Statistical Account of Scotland, collection of reports on the way people
      were living at the end of the eighteenth century in Scotland
strathspey, Scottish dance
suburbs, districts at the edge of a city
summa, total
syllabub, sweet frothy dish
terminated, closed
uniform, unvarying
virginals, spinet
Writers to the Signet, ancient and exclusive society of Scottish solicitors
wynd, lane in town in Scotland
yeomanry, volunteer force of cavalry

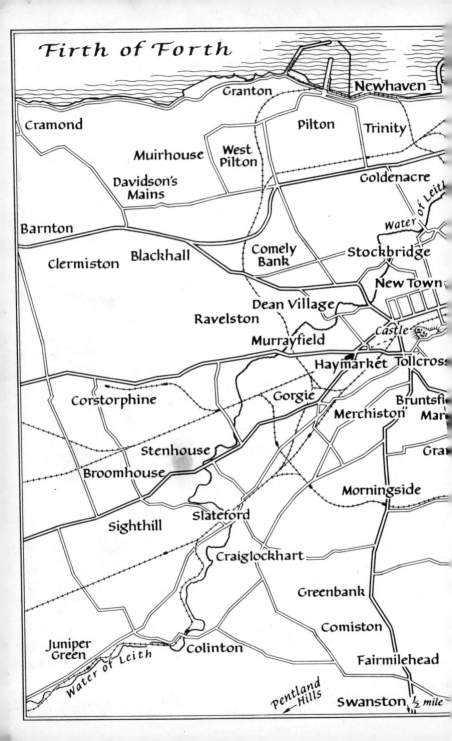

Firth of Forth

Newhaven
Granton
Cramond
Pilton
Trinity
Muirhouse
West
Pilton
Goldenacre
Davidson's
Mains
Water of Leith
Barnton
Comely
Bank
Stockbridge
Clermiston
Blackhall
New Town
Dean Village
Castle
Ravelston
Murrayfield
Haymarket
Tollcross
Gorgie
Bruntsfi
Corstorphine
Merchiston
Mar
Stenhouse
Gra
Broomhouse
Morningside
Sighthill
Slateford
Craiglockhart
Greenbank
Comiston
Juniper
Green
Colinton
Fairmilehead
Water of Leith
Pentland
Hills
Swanston ½ mile